BECOMING GOD'S
TRUE WOMAN

NANCY LEIGH DEMOSS
editor

BECOMING GOD'S
TRUE WOMAN

CROSSWAY BOOKS
WHEATON, ILLINOIS

PDF ISBN: 978-1-4335-0549-2

Mobipocket ISBN: 978-1-4335-0550-8

Library of Congress Cataloging-in-Publication Data
[Biblical womanhood in the home]
   Becoming God's true woman / Nancy Leigh DeMoss, editor.
  — 2nd ed.
     p. cm.
    Includes indexes.
    ISBN 13: 978-1-4335-0366-5 (tpb)
    1. Christian women—Religious life. 2. Women—Biblical teaching.
  I. DeMoss, Nancy Leigh. II. Title.
BV4527.B56   2008
248.8'43—dc22   2008032935

VP		17	16	15	14	13	12	11	10	09	08
14	13	12	11	10	9	8	7	6	5	4	3	2	1

To our daughters—
both physical and spiritual.

May your lives always adorn the Gospel of Christ.
May you know the joy of being true women of God.
And may your homes be reflections of His great
redemptive heart and plan.

CONTENTS

ACKNOWLEDGMENTS

EACH CONTRIBUTOR TO THIS BOOK has been encouraged and assisted in multiple ways on this project by individuals that include husbands, staff, friends, and other fellow servants. Space does not permit us to identify those individuals by name, but from our hearts, each of us says "thank you" for your prayers, input, and practical assistance.

We also owe a collective "thank you" to:

Council on Biblical Manhood and Womanhood (CBMW) and FamilyLife (FL)—the two ministries that cohosted the Building Strong Families in Your Church conference in March 2000, where these messages were first presented as workshop sessions.

Wayne Grudem (then-President of CBMW) and Dennis Rainey (Executive Director of FL) for your leadership of these strategic ministries and for your faithfulness in lifting high the flag of Truth in a day when it takes great courage to do so. We thank God for giving such men to the church and pray that He will grant you favor and multiply your efforts for His glory.

Crossway Books and Lane Dennis (president) for your bold commitment to the Truth and for your vision for publishing this series. Thank you for prayerfully considering what needs to be said to the church in the twenty-first century, and for your efforts to penetrate the darkness with the magnificent light of His ways.

Ted Griffin—you are a true servant of the Lord and of His people. Thank you for taking on the thankless tasks of reviewing, editing, and helping to shape this book and for compiling the indices that have made it an even more useful resource.

Soli Deo Gloria.

CONTRIBUTORS

NANCY LEIGH DEMOSS is the host and teacher for *Revive Our Hearts* and *Seeking Him*, two nationally syndicated radio programs heard weekdays on some 1,000 radio outlets. Since 1979 she has served on the staff of Life Action Ministries in Niles, Michigan. She has shared her burden for personal and corporate revival in conferences and retreats throughout North America and abroad. Nancy is a best-selling author. Her books include: *Choosing Forgiveness*; *A Place of Quiet Rest*; *Lies Women Believe: And the Truth that Sets Them Free*; *A Thirty-Day Walk with God in the Psalms*; and the *Revive Our Hearts Trilogy*: *Brokenness: The Heart God Revives*; *Surrender: The Heart God Controls*; and *Holiness: The Heart God Purifies*. She is also the co-author of *Lies Young Women Believe* and *Seeking Him*, an interactive Bible study on revival.

BARBARA HUGHES supported her husband Kent's pastoral ministry for 41 years while raising four children. They have 21 grandchildren. Barbara is a popular teacher of women's groups and numerous Bible studies. She is the author of *Disciplines of a Godly Woman*, which encourages spiritual disciplines as a lifeline to a meaningful relationship with God. Barbara also co-authored three books with her husband: *Common Sense Parenting*, *Liberating Ministry from the Success Syndrome*, and *Disciplines of a Godly Family*.

SUSAN HUNT, a pastor's wife, is a mother and grandmother, and a consultant to Presbyterian Church in America's Women in the Church Ministry. She holds a degree in Christian education from Columbia Theological Seminary. Susan's burden for women, and especially biblical womanhood, is clear in her many books, which include: *The True Woman*; *Heirs of the Covenant*; *By Design: God's Distinctive Calling for Women*; *Spiritual Mothering: The Titus 2*

Mandate for Women Mentoring Women; and *Your Home—A Place of Grace*. Susan co-authored *The Legacy of Biblical Womanhood* and wrote two children's books, including *My ABC Bible Verses*. Susan is a member of the Council on Biblical Manhood and Womanhood, and co-authored with Ligon Duncan *Women's Ministry in the Local Church*.

MARY KASSIAN, founder and president of *Alabaster Flask Ministries*, challenges women to pursue God with passion and delight in his design. A wife and mother of three sons, Mary is also an internationally known speaker and Bible teacher and a member of the Council on Biblical Manhood and Womanhood. She is distinguished professor of women's studies at The Southern Baptist Theological Seminary in Louisville. Mary is the author of several books and videos including: *The Feminist Mistake: The Radical Impact of Feminism on Church and Culture*; *Women, Creation, and the Fall*; *In My Father's House: Finding Your Heart's True Home*; and *Conversation Peace: Improve Your Relationships One Word at a Time*.

CAROLYN MAHANEY is the wife of C. J. Mahaney who leads Sovereign Grace Ministries. A homemaker, mother of four, and grandmother of seven, Carolyn also speaks to women at conferences and churches. She and her three married daughters communicate on biblical womanhood and other women's issues through a daily blog called "Girl Talk." Carolyn is the author of *Feminine Appeal: Seven Virtues of a Godly Wife and Mother*; *Girl Talk: Mother-Daughter Conversations on Biblical Womanhood*; and *Shopping for Time: How to Do It All and Not Be Overwhelmed*. She also wrote a section for wives in her husband's book *Sex, Romance, and the Glory of God*.

DOROTHY KELLEY PATTERSON is an active mother, grandmother, and homemaker, and a frequent speaker and Bible teacher at women's conferences. She is professor of theology in women's studies at Southwestern Theological Seminary in Fort Worth, Texas, where her husband, Paige Patterson, is president. She is a member of the Biblical Council on Manhood and Womanhood. As an accomplished writer of books and articles, Dr. Patterson is the author of *The Family: Unchanging Principles for Changing Times*; *BeAttitudes For Women*; *A Woman Seeking God*; *A Handbook for Parents in Ministry*; *A Handbook for Minister's Wives*; and *Where's Mom? The High Calling of Wives and Mothers*. She is also the General Editor for *The Woman's Study Bible*.

P. BUNNY WILSON and her husband, Frank, have been married since 1973. They have six children and live in Southern California. She is founder and president of *New Dawn Productions*. A gifted author, counselor, speaker, and teacher, she has appeared on numerous national radio and television programs, including *The Oprah Winfrey Show*; *The 700 Club*; *Woman to Woman*; *Beverly LaHaye Live*; *Today's Family*; *USA Radio Network*; and others. Bunny is the author of *Liberated Through Submission*; *Betrayal's Baby*; *Knight in Shining Armor*; *The Master's Degree: Majoring in Your Marriage*; *Seven Secrets Women Want to Know*; *Night Come Swiftly*; and the series *Are You Looking for God?*

INTRODUCTION

Nancy Leigh DeMoss

IN 1990 *TIME MAGAZINE* devoted an entire special issue to the subject of women.[1] The managing editor's column began:

> As roughly half the world's population, women would hardly seem to need to struggle for attention. Yet struggle is precisely what they have been doing in the final decades of the 20th century. Their endeavors deserve no less a word than revolution—in expectations, accomplishments, self-realization and relationships with men. It is a revolution that, though far from complete, promises over time to bring about changes as profound for men and women as any that have occurred in Eastern Europe or the Soviet Union in the past year.[2]

The eighty-six-page special issue included articles on such revolutionary developments as "the road to equality," the psychology of growing up female, the changing roles of women in the workforce, women as consumers, changing views on marriage and family, and the hurdles women face in pursuing political careers.

One section featured profiles of "10 tough-minded women" who have combined "talent and drive" to become "successful" in their careers: the police chief of a major metropolitan police force, a baseball owner, a rap artist, an AIDS activist, a rock climber, a bishop in a mainline denomination, a fashion tycoon, a saxophonist, an Indian chief, and a choreographer. These women were lauded chiefly for their success in their chosen vocations.

Conspicuous by its absence throughout the issue was any recognition given to women who have succeeded in ways not tied to careers—women who have successfully stayed married to the same man or who have succeeded in bringing up children who are making a positive contribution to society. Not surprisingly, no bouquets were handed out to women for being reverent and temperate or modest and chaste or gentle and quiet, for loving their husbands and children, for keeping a clean, well-ordered home, for caring for elderly parents, for providing hospitality, for acts of kindness, service, and mercy, or for demonstrating compassion for the poor and needy—the kind of success that, according to the Word of God, is what women should aspire to attain (1 Tim. 5:10; Titus 2:3–5).

I was struck by the fact that though *Time*'s coverage featured women in many different roles and settings, there were precious few references to home. (The few references to marriage and family highlighted "single women who are choosing to be unmarried . . . with children,"[3] stay-at-home dads, divorced moms, lesbians, and working moms—all evidence of the pervasiveness of this revolution that recognizes all lifestyles as equally valid choices, except perhaps those women who choose to center their hearts and lives around their families. Women readers who have chosen a career as homemakers could easily have been shaken by the solitary sidebar article on wives entitled "Caution: Hazardous Work." The subheading read: "Looking for lifelong economic security? Don't bank on homemaking."[4]

My intent in this context is not so much to address the issue of women and careers as to point out the extent to which the identity and value of women has come to be equated with their role in the community or in the marketplace. That is how their worth is defined, measured, and experienced. By contrast, relatively little priority or value is assigned to their role in the home.

As I read commentaries such as that provided by *Time*, I feel deep sadness over what has been forfeited in the midst of this revolution—the beauty, the wonder, and the treasure of the distinctive makeup, calling, and mission of women.

It should come as no huge surprise that the secular world is confused and off-base about the identity and calling of women. But what I find distressing is the extent to which the revolution described above has taken hold even within the evangelical world.

We see the fruit of that revolution as prominent Christian speakers, authors, and leaders promote an agenda, whether subtly or overtly, that encourages women to define and discover their worth in the workplace, in society, or at church, while minimizing (or even at the expense of) their distinctive roles in the home as daughters, sisters, wives, and mothers—as bearers and nurturers of life, as caregivers, as those privileged and responsible to shape the heart and character of the next generation.

The feminist revolution was supposed to bring women greater fulfillment and freedom. It was supposed to make us feel better about ourselves; after all, "You've come a long way, baby!" But we see the poisoned fruit of the revolution in the eyes and pitiable cries of women who are drowning in the quagmire of serial divorce and remarriage and wayward children; women who are utterly exhausted from the demands of trying to juggle one or more jobs, function as single parents, and be active at church; women who are disoriented and confused, who lack a sense of mission, vision, and purpose for their lives and who are perpetually, pathetically shrouded in wound-edness, self-doubt, resentment, and guilt.

Yes, the revolution has come to church. And when you add up all the gains and losses, there is no question in my mind that women have been the losers—as have their husbands and their children and grandchildren—as has the entire church—as has our lost, unbelieving culture.

Some years ago a fresh sense of mission began to stir within my heart. Since that time, the sense of pessimism and hopelessness, of being swallowed up by the revolution, has been replaced by rich hope and excitement.

A study of the development of modern feminism (feminism itself actually dates back to the garden of Eden) impressed me with the fact that this massive revolution did not begin as a massive revolution. It started in the hearts of a relatively small handful of women with an agenda, women who were determined and intentional in their efforts; it started with a few seminal books and speeches; it spread throughout the living rooms of America (which is where women were at the time) until it became a groundswell; it spread by painting for women a picture (deceptive as it was) of their plight and creating a vision of how things could be different; it ignited indignation, longing, and hope in women's hearts; it sparked a refusal to be content with the status quo.

As I pondered these things, I began to wonder what might happen in our day if even a small number of devoted, intentional women would begin to pray and believe God for a revolution of a different kind—a *counterrevolution*—within the evangelical world. What would happen if a "remnant" of women were willing to repent, to return to the authority of God's Word, to embrace God's priorities and purpose for their lives and homes, and to live out the beauty and the wonder of womanhood as God created it to be?

Of course, I realize that such women will always be in the minority (as were the early feminists). But as this inner compulsion has grown, I have taken courage from the promise that "one . . . of you puts to flight a thousand, since it is the LORD your God who fights for you, just as he promised you" (Josh. 23:10). I have come to believe that the measure of success is not whether we "win" the war (for we know that in the end, this battle has already been won), but whether we are willing to "wage" the war.

You need to understand that I am not a fighter by nature. The older I get, the more I crave a simple, uncomplicated, anonymous lifestyle. I had a natural reluctance to jump into what I knew would be a lifetime of going against the flow (even in the church); I didn't relish the idea of being politically incorrect all the time. But greater than my fears and reservations is a passion for the glory of God. And God is glorified through thankful, trusting, obedient, compassionate, serving, virtuous, joyful, feminine women who reflect to our world the heart and character of the Lord Jesus himself. As we are filled with his Spirit, we radiate his beauty and make the gospel believable.

Unlike most revolutions, this counterrevolution does not require that we march in the streets or send letters to Congress or join yet another organization. It does not require us to leave our homes; in fact, for many women, it calls them back into their homes. It requires only that we humble ourselves, that we learn, affirm, and live out the biblical pattern of womanhood, and that we teach the ways of God to the next generation. It is a revolution that will take place on our knees.

As I have come to accept God's call to be a part of this counterrevolution, I have discovered that I am not alone. Everywhere I have shared this vision, I have found that "deep answers to deep"; the call to return to biblical womanhood resonates within Christian women who have tasted the bitter fruit of the feminist revolution and who know within their hearts that God's ways are right.

Further, I have met a number of women who are serious students of the Word and are particularly gifted at communicating God's plan for our lives as women. What a joy it was to sit and share with some of those women at the conference on *Building Strong Families in Your Church* cohosted in March 2000 by FamilyLife and the Council on Biblical Manhood and Womanhood. Our hearts beat alike for the glory of God to be seen in our homes and churches as women embrace their God-given calling.

The women who led workshops at that conference, and whose messages are presented here in written form, represent a variety of backgrounds and life experiences. They approach the subject of biblical womanhood in the home from a number of different angles and teaching styles. But there runs throughout a thread of delight with the greatness of God's created order and the part we as women play in his grand redemptive plan.

These women join me in inviting you to become a part of this counterrevolution—waged not with the weapons of anger, discontent, rebellion, and rancor, but with humility, obedience, love, and prayer—believing that in God's time, the changes that result will indeed be more profound and on a higher order than any of the massive sociopolitical changes our world has experienced in this generation.

Though not written in the context of the topic at hand, this prayer by John Greenleaf Whittier captures something of the heart of this book and of the movement we are believing God to birth anew in our day:

Dear Lord and Father of mankind,
Forgive our foolish ways!
Reclothe us in our rightful mind;
In purer lives Thy service find,
In deeper reverence, praise.

In simple trust like theirs who heard,
Beside the Syrian sea,
The gracious calling of the Lord,
Let us, like them, without a word,
Rise up and follow Thee.

Drop Thy still dews of quietness
Till all our strivings cease.
Take from our souls the strain and stress,
And let our ordered lives confess
The beauty of Thy peace.

PART ONE

The Glory of Womanhood as Created by God

FEMININITY: DEVELOPING A BIBLICAL PERSPECTIVE

Carolyn Mahaney

WHEN MY OLDEST DAUGHTER, Nicole, got married, she chose a unique theme for her wedding: her favorite Shakespeare play, *Much Ado About Nothing*. In addition to the Italian Renaissance decor of maypoles, wreaths, and kissing balls, the theme was carried on through to the reception, where guests were treated to four scenes from the play by the drama team from our church. Though written at the close of the sixteenth century, the witty sparring between the sharp-tongued, independent Beatrice and her reluctant love interest, Benedick, is as timeless as any modern romantic comedy:

> Beatrice: I wonder that you will still be talking, Signior Benedick: nobody marks you.
> Benedick: What, my dear Lady Disdain! Are you yet living?
> Beatrice: Is it possible disdain should die while she hath such meet food to feed it as Signior Benedick? Courtesy itself must convert to disdain, if you come into her presence.[1]

Though the language is archaic, Shakespeare's keen observation of the War of the Sexes is as fresh today as when he wrote it. The acerbic Beatrice, or "Lady Disdain" as Benedick aptly calls her, is still celebrated in our culture. She's a woman who contends with the men in her life and who is disrespectful in words and actions. Sadly, this is the model many young women grow up emulating.

While I'm glad Nicole enjoys Shakespeare's classic play, I'm more pleased that she has a biblical view of womanhood. Without God's Word as an anchor, modern women drift to extremes— either embracing caricatures of femininity or rejecting it altogether. Secular feminist Susan Brownmiller sums up the confusion in her book *Femininity*: "Women are all female impersonators to some degree."[2] Ms. Brownmiller's definition of femininity is also alarming. "Femininity, in essence, is a romantic sentiment, a nostalgic tradition of imposed limitations," she writes.[3]

The Bible gives women far greater honor, hope, and freedom than this definition of femininity. We don't have to impersonate anyone, much less suffer limitations. The Scriptures that speak of women and godly femininity are infused with dignity and purpose. The God who created femininity has a beautiful purpose and plan for women.

CREATED FEMININE

Look back with me to the inauguration of femininity at the dawn of creation. The language of Genesis is elegantly simple:

> So God created man in his own image, in the image of God he created him; male and female he created them. . . . So the LORD God caused a deep sleep to fall upon the man, and while he slept took one of his ribs and closed up its place with flesh. And the rib that the LORD God had taken from the man he made into a woman and brought her to the man. (Gen. 1:27; 2:21–22)

This passage shows that woman was the beautiful handiwork of God our Creator. Woman was God's idea, his creation. In fact, as we read the whole account of God's brilliant creation production, we discover that the woman was the finishing design of all that he created. She was the last act. Dare we say that God left the best for last? (I don't think we can take too much pride in that fact when we remember who was the first to eat the forbidden fruit!)

The important point here is that *God* created us, and being the creation of God determines everything for us as women. We don't look to our culture to find our feminine identity; we don't consult our feelings to discover our purpose. Everything that we are and everything that we do must be rooted in God.

It's not mere chance that we are women—our gender is not accidental. We were intentionally and purposefully created. We are the planned and foreordained determination of an all-wise, all-powerful, and all-loving God.

That means when God created the first woman, he made a fully feminine creature. You and I did not become feminine because someone gave us a doll and put a dress on us—we were born feminine because we were *created* feminine.

The feminist doctrine of our time upholds the notion that femininity is a matter of cultural conditioning. Many feminists argue that the only essential difference between men and women is our anatomy, but Genesis teaches otherwise. Because God created male and female, we women are innately feminine. Granted, a woman can accentuate her femininity or she can detract from it, but she cannot change it—our sex chromosomes are in every cell of our bodies. Our femininity is a gift of grace from a loving God.

CALLED TO BE A HELPER

In the garden, God made man and woman fellow stewards of creation but with different, divinely assigned roles. "Then the LORD God said, 'It is not good that the man should be alone; I will make him a helper fit for him'" (Gen. 2:18). That is why God created Eve from Adam. She was created to be a helper suitable to him, to complement him, to nourish him, and to help him in the task that God had given him. Paul summarizes the creation plan by saying: "For man was not made from woman, but woman from man. Neither was man created for woman, but woman for man" (1 Cor. 11:8–9). This unique feminine purpose is well defined by John Piper: "At the heart of mature femininity is a freeing disposition to affirm, receive, and nurture strength and leadership from worthy men in ways appropriate to a woman's differing relationships."[4]

Note the phrase "differing relationships." It is not only in the context of marriage that we can express our femininity. We were created feminine; that is not a state conferred in marriage. We do not wait until we reach the marriage altar to give full expression to our femininity. Though it looks slightly different when we are single than when we are married, all women are called to display their femininity in a variety of relationships.

Please don't misunderstand me. This doesn't mean that we allow men to lead us into sin or away from God's priorities in our lives. But it means that we are *inclined* to affirm the leadership and initiative of the men around us.

Single women, please enjoy (appropriately) being a helper in these differing relationships with men, and trust God for your future. I encourage you to be at peace in this season. If the Lord has marriage planned for you, then you can rest assured that he is also the perfect matchmaker. It was God who said it was not good for the man to be alone. We have no record that Adam had complained of any lack. Rather, it was God who declared that aloneness is not good for a man. God was the one who made man aware of his need for a woman. So even though in your life there may be single men who seem to be unaware of their need for a woman, *God is aware*. Just as he did with Adam, God can break into the life of that single man and make him realize his desire for companionship. Resting in this truth will free you from the temptation to manipulate, complain, or become bitter—three traits that greatly tarnish the luster of femininity.

In all our relationships, we should be making room for godly men to practice servant leadership. But I would especially encourage single women to ask the Lord to give them creative ways to inspire men to lead. Granted, this is not always easy, and I'm not promising you that all men will automatically lead. What matters is that you are cultivating the habit of making room for the leadership of the men in your life.

There are men in your life that the Lord has provided in this season—fathers, bosses, friends—and they need to know that you "incline" toward them, instead of resisting them in a stiff-necked posture of the heart. You encourage their godly leadership when you seek their counsel before making your own decisions. You respect them when you avoid sinfully complaining to others about their actions or decisions and resist publicly questioning their actions. When appropriate, we should ask questions, respectfully disagree, and offer our counsel. But we have to guard our hearts lest we allow our culture's attitude of female disrespect for all things male to permeate our perspective on their leadership. If you're not sure how well you are doing in this area, ask the men in your life.

DOES THIS HELP MY HUSBAND?

If you are a married woman, the Lord calls you to express your femininity more particularly in the context of marriage. In some ways, this is much the same call as for single women, but it is more specifically defined and directed toward your husband. You display your femininity by coming alongside your husband and helping him in the task that God has given him. Author Douglas Wilson provides a wonderful portrait of a godly, complementary marriage:

> The man needs the help; the woman needs to help. Marriage was created by God to provide a companionship in the labor of dominion. The cultural mandate, the requirement to fill and subdue the earth, is still in force, and a husband cannot fulfill this portion of the task in isolation. He needs a companion suitable for him in the work to which God has called him. He is called to the work and must receive help from her. She is called to the work through ministering to him. He is oriented to the task, and she is oriented to him.[5]

Wives, we all have the same job description: We are our husband's helper. If you are wondering whether to pursue some particular endeavor, ask yourself this important question: *Does this help my husband?* Usually that one simple question will make your decision clear. My problem is that all too often I forget to ask that question. In fact, I have to confess that my orientation is often really toward myself rather than toward my husband. On numerous occasions I have made choices or pursued opportunities that served me rather than my husband.

This tendency is frequently illustrated in the mundane tasks of life. Recently I was cleaning out several disorganized cabinets in my kitchen. As I was working, I remembered the bathroom cabinet, which was also in dire need of cleaning. On several occasions as my husband had rummaged around that disheveled bathroom cabinet, he had graciously asked me when I thought I could get to that project. I usually informed him that I just didn't have time at present, but that

I would get to it as soon as I could. However, as I was cleaning out the kitchen cabinets that day, I realized the problem was not that I didn't have the time to clean the bathroom cabinet; the truth was that I didn't really care about the bathroom cabinet. I wanted the kitchen cabinets clean because that served *my* purposes. My orientation was not directed toward my husband and his preferences—it was directed toward me.

My selfish orientation has not only been evident in the way I care for my home; it has been highlighted in other areas as well. On one occasion God exposed it when I offered to make a meal for a friend in need. Of course that sounds like a noble endeavor, but I volunteered without asking my husband or even considering whether this activity would be considerate of him. I just proceeded with my own plan because it seemed good to me. When my husband discovered that I had offered to make a meal for my friend, he lovingly pointed out that it was not a good time for me to be serving in this way. It was a season in which we had many other responsibilities, with lots of traveling and speaking engagements. I was not serving my husband and my family by adding another task to our hectic lives at that moment.

As I reflected on the situation, I realized that I had agreed to make the meal because I wanted to look good in the eyes of my friend. I wanted her to know I was just as good a friend as every other woman who was bringing her a meal. Had she known what our schedule and responsibilities were at that time, I'm sure she would have dissuaded me from this task. But that wasn't a consideration for me—I was seeking to impress her. After confessing my self-promoting pride to both God and my husband, I ended up buying my friend a meal from a restaurant. However, this could have been avoided if I had asked, *Does this help my husband?* I could have quickly determined that making a meal for my friend that particular week was not a wise thing to do.

Wives, in light of the Lord's instruction to us, we have to ask ourselves the hard questions on a regular basis: Do I care for my home in a way that helps my husband or serves me? Do I manage my time in a manner that assists my husband or serves my own agenda? Does the way I serve others support my husband or promote me? Do I ask for my husband's input before committing myself to a plan? Am I oriented to him and the work to which God has called him? We honor the Lord when we minister to our husbands in ways that enhance our God-given roles as companions and helpers.

MADE TO NURTURE

I remember sitting next to a woman on an airplane flight who was addressing envelopes. We struck up a conversation, and she told me she was sending out wedding invitations for one daughter and graduation invitations for the other. I was about to congratulate her when she admitted, "It's so nice to be getting rid of both of them at the same time."

I cringed when I heard that. I was thankful her daughters weren't there to hear her words. Though it's a common attitude for many women in our culture, it should not characterize us as Christians. God intends that we enjoy motherhood and delight in our children.

As women, we are created to be life bearers. Our bodies have been designed with the ability to mother—to receive, carry, and bear young. In fact, our bodies prepare themselves repeatedly to conceive and bear young. We express our femininity by gratefully embracing every stage of childbearing, receiving and nurturing each child as a gracious gift from God.

In no way does this exclude single women. As Elisabeth Elliot reminds us, a single woman may mother many children: "She *can* have children! She may be a spiritual mother, as was Amy Carmichael, by the offering of her singleness, transformed for the good of far more children than a natural mother may produce. All is received and made holy by the One to whom it is offered."[6]

Single and childless married women alike can express their femininity by nurturing other people's children. When you babysit, you are giving expression to your femininity. When you take an interest and reach out to other people's children, you are displaying your God-given femininity. When you tutor children or sponsor a needy child internationally or volunteer at a crisis pregnancy center or build relationships with your nieces or nephews, you are bearing fruit in this area. I give thanks to God for all the single women in my life and for the countless times they have cared for my children, loving them as though they were their very own. We mothers want to say thank you for their doing that, for their blessing us in that way. It means so much to us, and we are grateful to them. But they are doing more than blessing us; they are honoring God by selflessly investing in the young lives around them.

MOTHERHOOD MELTDOWNS

If we do have children, we bring delight to God when we find joy in our roles as mothers. But what about those times when we find this mothering task to be a burden? What about those times when we lack joy or feel overwhelmed with the endless demands? Motherhood is a huge responsibility, an enormous task. In fact, there is probably no profession that requires greater sacrifice and servanthood. There is nothing easy about good mothering. As one woman said, "It can be back-breaking, heart-wrenching, and anxiety-producing—and that's just the morning!" It's easy to grow weary and to focus on all the sacrifices being made rather than on the joys that motherhood can bring.

I vividly remember one particular weekend when I hit motherhood meltdown. My two older daughters were five and four and my youngest was still an infant, and C. J. was away on a ministry trip. The older girls came down with a vicious stomach virus, and I spent a solid twenty-four-hour period cleaning up behind them. Of course, they missed the bucket nearly every time. I was simultaneously cleaning up vomit, changing dirty diapers, and doing endless loads of soiled laundry. There was no relief, and I was utterly exhausted. I remember thinking, *Really, is what I'm doing all that important? There are women out there working 9 to 5 who seem to be doing something much more important than this!* It was a discouraging and emotionally depleting time.

When C. J. returned, he sent me out for my morning away, a weekly habit for us. I took my Bible and holed up in the corner of a nearby fast-food restaurant, desperately seeking God for a fresh vision for the work of mothering. As I prayed and studied God's Word, the Lord revealed to me that I wasn't "just" to be a mom; rather, God had *called* me to be a mother. The perspective of having a calling gave motherhood a whole new significance, and I repented of my complaining and grumbling.

It is common for weary mothers to lack biblical perspective, to need fresh vision for the significance of our calling. In those moments, there really is no other source of refreshment than God. I would encourage you to offer your weariness and discouragement to Jesus in prayer, trusting his intercession on your behalf. Only your Creator can provide you with the eternal perspective you need to see these fleeting years as vitally important in the lives of your children. God wants to give you fresh strength and new joy for the task, which he is more than able to provide from the riches of his grace that he lavishes on us "in all wisdom and insight" (Eph. 1:7-8).

A LOVE FOR THE HOME

The woman of virtue portrayed in Proverbs 31 is commended for watching over the affairs of her household. In Titus 2:3–5, Paul instructs the older women to teach younger women how to be busy at home. These and other Scriptures make it clear that while it is the man's responsibility to be the provider for the home, it is the woman's responsibility to be the caretaker for the home. Domesticity—devotion to the quality of home life—is an essential facet of femininity.

Single women (especially young women), may I advise you not to wait until marriage to cultivate this? Whether you get married or not, you can express your femininity by developing a love and devotion for the home. In fact, don't assume that if you ignore cultivating a heart for the home while you are single, you will automatically have it once you get married. You may be in for a surprise! I have talked to many married women who admitted they didn't value domesticity when they got married. They didn't like *being* at home; they didn't like *caring* for the home. They didn't value homemaking as a worthy profession. Why? Because they didn't develop a vision for the importance of home life while they were single. They filled their single years with every possible pursuit *but* a devotion to the home. I'm not saying other pursuits are wrong; the single years do provide opportunities for many other God-honoring pursuits. But these should be balanced with cultivating a love for the home.

Whether you are living at home with your parents or you have a home of your own, there are some practical steps you can take to learn domesticity. Learn now how to manage the order and cleanliness of a home, how to cook meals and care for clothing, and how to beautify a home.

Even for older singles, there is still a godly call on your life as a woman to bring balance to your professional life by "working at home" (Titus 2:5). I know many single women who have created warm, appealing homes—whatever their living arrangements—and who regularly practice hospitality. Some keep guest books or photo albums of those who have shared a meal or stayed overnight in their homes; others are talented with crafts, filling their rooms with beautiful, handmade items. Marital status has nothing to do with the feminine desire to create a warm, inviting home.

There are many practical aspects to consider in homemaking. In 1 Timothy 5:14, Paul commands young widows to "manage," or preside over, their homes. We are to manage the order or schedule of the home, its cleanliness, and its atmosphere, as well as to engage in other practical acts of service such as preparing meals and meeting the clothing needs of our families.

Proverbs 14:1 says, "The wisest of women builds her house, but folly with her own hands tears it down." In other words, the home is our place to build. Our culture says it's not a place worthy of our best labors, but we have to be careful not to allow the world to affect our thinking. The home is our primary place for ministry. Someone once said of Edith Schaeffer, "As many people were brought to the Lord through Mrs. Schaeffer's cinnamon buns as through Dr. Schaeffer's sermons."[7] Our scope of ministry is different than that of men, but it is no less important—it is God's assignment to us.

THE WITNESS OF FEMININITY

We were created purposefully by God to live purposefully by his Word. Though the world, even classic literature, would memorialize the tongue and attitude of "Lady Disdain," Christian women can be different by the power of the Holy Spirit. We do not have to be "female impersonators" who view femininity as a "nostalgic tradition of imposed limitations." Contrary to popular opinion, femininity is not "much ado about nothing"! In the awe-inspiring generosity of the Lord, we have been created with a unique task to be fulfilled in order to glorify him. If we cultivate and express our femininity with this in view, we will be commended by our Maker for the wise stewardship of this precious gift.

TRUE BEAUTY

Carolyn Mahaney

YOU MAY HAVE HEARD IT SAID that one of the differences between a man and a woman is that when a man looks at himself in the mirror, he admires the one physical feature about himself that's attractive, while a woman only sees the features she considers unattractive.

I can't verify that this is true of men, but it certainly seems true about women. Whether real or imagined, our eyes hone in on our "imperfections." We see the blemish. We compare ourselves to the world's current ideal of beauty and always come up short.

Today's woman faces intense pressure to conform to a perfect physical ideal. Is it any wonder so many go to drastic measures to change their bodies? A recent study indicated that American women spent a *half-billion* dollars in one year on shape-enhancing garments. In 2000 the American Society of Plastic Surgeons indicated that cosmetic surgery procedures among women had increased by a dramatic 165 percent. The top five cosmetic surgeries for women are liposuction, breast augmentation, eyelid surgery, facelift, and tummy tuck—with no end in sight for the demand.[1] From Argentina to Japan, women of every culture are submitting with increasing frequency to the knife. In Mexico nose jobs are the status gift for girls celebrating their *quinceanera*, the traditional coming-of-age fifteenth birthday party. Just over the border, their California peers are getting breast augmentation procedures as a high school graduation gift.[2]

The Glory of Womanhood

This isn't a new trend. Author Robin Marantz Henig provides this historical overview of the price of perfection:

> Over the centuries, women have mauled and manipulated just about every body part—lips, eyes, ears, waists, skulls, foreheads, feet—that did not quite fit into the cookie-cutter ideal of a particular era's fashion. In China, almost up until World War II, upper-class girls had their feet bound, crippling them for life but ensuring the three- or four-inch-long feet that were prized as exquisitely feminine. In central Africa, the Mangbettu wrapped the heads of female infants in pieces of giraffe hide to attain the elongated, cone-shaped heads that were taken to be a sign of beauty and intelligence. During the Renaissance, well-born European women plucked out hairs, one by one, from their natural hairlines all the way back to the crown of their heads, to give themselves the high, rounded foreheads thought beautiful at the time. . . .
>
> Among the Padaung people of early-twentieth-century Burma, the ideal of female beauty involved a greatly elongated neck, preferably fifteen inches or more. This was accomplished by fitting girls with a series of brass neck rings. At a very young age, girls began by wearing five rings; by the time they were fully grown they were wearing as many as twenty-four, piled one on top of another. . . .
>
> The weight of the rings leads to crushed collarbones and broken ribs, and the vertebrae in the neck become stretched and floppy. Indeed, these women wear the rings round-the-clock because, without them, their stretched-out necks are too weak to support their heads.[3]

The author goes on to capture the frenzied search for ideal female beauty. Overweight women in England in the 1600s were bled; chic women in the 1930s swallowed tapeworms. Queen Elizabeth I, in search of porcelain skin, used a potentially deadly combination of vinegar and lead that resulted in the total corrosion of her skin. Ancient Egyptian women used drops of antimony sulfide to make their eyes glitter, eventually destroying their vision. Victorian women summoned their maids to tight-lace them into corsets, cutting off their oxygen and displacing internal organs in order to achieve an eighteen-inch waist. Flappers in the 1920s folded their breasts to simulate a fashionably flat torso or used constricting devices like the one from the Boyish Form Brassiere Company.

That might sound quite primitive until you consider the relatively recent recall of silicone implants that had been inserted into the chests of more than a million American women. Silicone wasn't much of an improvement over the materials used by an early cosmetic surgeon named Charles Miller in 1903. By Miller's own account, he was opening women's chests and inserting "braided silk, bits of silk floss, particles of celluloid, vegetable ivory and several other foreign materials."[4]

DIGITAL DRESS-UP

The temptation for women to be preoccupied with their physical appearance has always existed. However, it appears that contemporary women are more driven in their pursuit of physical beauty than ever before. Blitzed by the media, we are presented continuously with voices and images that define what we are to look like. In previous centuries, women might have compared themselves with the other ten women in their village; today women compare themselves with pictures of the supermodels put on display by the worldwide fashion industry. That image of beauty is so narrow in its range that most women feel unattractive in comparison.

Even worse is the deception in the fashion industry itself. Did you know that most of the models we see in the magazines don't even look like their *own* pictures? Fashion magazine editors admit that almost every photograph of a model has been digitally altered. So think about it: this alluring model has been toned by her personal trainer, had her hair done by a professional stylist, her face painted by a professional makeup artist, and her image captured by a professional photographer under ideal lighting. After this, if the model *still* doesn't look good enough, she is recast through computer graphics.

CRAVINGS FROM THE HEART

This begs the question, why? Why are women so obsessed with physical beauty? Why would women go to such extremes to be beautiful as culturally defined? Why aren't we pleased with "normal"?

The answer is simple and sobering: our hearts are full of evil desires and sinful lusts. And to differing degrees our hearts have believed the lie that physical beauty will bring satisfaction and recognition. You know the false promises: *If you're beautiful, you will be happy and successful. You will be popular among the women, and you will be desirable to the men. You will know lasting intimacy and true love. You will be confident and secure. You will be important and significant.*

These are all things our sinful hearts crave. We lust for success, recognition, significance, importance, and approval. We become obsessed with making ourselves physically beautiful in an attempt to satisfy these sinful cravings. Yet the message is a lie. Physical beauty doesn't ensure happiness, fulfillment, or success. We can validate this fact by observing the most physically attractive women in the world.

Consider Princess Diana. She was the most photographed woman in the world. She became a celebrity of unprecedented magnitude. Yet she lived a troubled life. Her fairy-tale marriage to Prince Charles ended in divorce. Her subsequent relationships with other men all ended unhappily. She admitted to persistent bouts of depression, chronic loneliness, ongoing bulimia, and even several suicide attempts. She went to a number of psychotherapists, all to no avail. Her life ended tragically when she was just thirty-six-years-old.

Physical beauty does not deliver as advertised. It does not produce the happiness and success that the beguiling voices in our society promise. Our culture puts forth a false standard of beauty and a false message about beauty, but ultimately the wickedness already resident in the human heart is what motivates us to believe such lies and pursue them.

GOD'S DEFINITION OF BEAUTY

We are exhorted in Romans 12:2 not to allow the world around us to squeeze us into its mold. We need to ask ourselves if we have been captivated by our culture's definition of beauty or God's. Do our thoughts and actions regarding our appearance reflect a cultural standard or a biblical standard? In order to answer these questions honestly, we need to understand God's perspective of beauty.

Scripture reveals the falsehood and the futility of the quest for physical beauty. "Charm is deceitful, and beauty is vain" (Prov. 31:30). *Charm* in the Hebrew means "bodily form." Form and beauty are two things that our culture esteems and pursues with fervor; yet God exposes our pursuit of the perfect figure and beauty to be idolatrous.

A survey of physically beautiful women in the Bible confirms the truth of Proverbs. Physical beauty is more often associated with trouble and temptation than with blessing and goodness. You will find many stories in the Old Testament of lying, cheating, stealing, murder, adultery, and idol-worship, all linked to the physical beauty of women. The accounts of Sarah (Gen. 12:11–20), Rebekah (Gen. 26:7–11), and Tamar (2 Sam. 13:1–20) are a few examples. Nowhere in the Bible are women instructed to wish for, ask for, or strive for physical beauty. Instead, God's Word warns us of the futility and deceitfulness of such a pursuit. Neither does the Bible portray physical beauty as a blessing for those who have it. Instead, it can actually create greater potential for being snared by sin (Prov. 6:23–26).

However, there is a kind of beauty that we are to pursue. First Peter 3:4–5 tells us, "Let your adorning be the hidden person of the heart with the imperishable beauty of a gentle and quiet spirit, which in God's sight is very precious. For this is how the holy women who hoped in God used to adorn themselves."

God's definition of beauty stands in stark contrast to the way our culture defines beauty. Our culture defines beauty by how we look on the outside. God defines beauty by what we are like on the inside.

Our culture puts forth a standard of beauty that is unattainable by most. God puts forth a standard of beauty to which we can all attain if we just respond to his work of grace in our lives.

Our culture encourages women to cultivate a beauty that is skin deep. God tells us to pursue an inner beauty of great worth.

Our culture encourages women to cultivate a beauty that will only last for a brief time. God encourages women to cultivate a beauty that will never fade and that will only grow more attractive with the passing of time.

Our culture calls us to cultivate a beauty that impresses others. God summons us to cultivate a beauty that is first and foremost for his eyes.

Our culture entices us to aspire to the beauty of the latest glamorous model or this season's most popular actress. God bids us to aspire to the beauty of the holy women in the past who put their hope in God.

Do you see the difference? The beauty our culture esteems may turn some heads, but the beauty God calls us to cultivate will make a lasting impact. When a physically attractive woman walks by, we notice—men particularly! But that's the end of it. Her beauty makes a fleeting, momentary impression. But a woman who cultivates inner beauty, who fears God and lives to serve others, makes a difference in people's lives. Her beauty makes a lasting impact on the lives she touches. Godly, inner beauty makes an indelible mark on the lives of others and glorifies God.

HEART CHECK

Which beauty are we seeking to cultivate? Are we intentionally cultivating inner beauty, or do we give more attention to the outward appearance? The way we think about and attend to our personal appearance is really a mirror of our hearts. By reflecting either godly motivations or selfish motivations, we reveal whether our priority is to cultivate inner beauty or outer beauty.

Here's a "heart check" test for the purpose of self-examination—questions to help us discern our thoughts, motives, and goals with regard to the issue of beauty. These questions have helped me to see that all too often my desire is for self-glory rather than God's glory. Ask yourself these questions:

1) Do I spend more time daily caring for my personal appearance than I do in Bible study, prayer, and worship?
2) Do I spend excessive money on clothes, hair, and makeup, or is it an amount that is God-honoring?
3) Do I want to lose weight to "feel better about myself," or do I desire to be self-disciplined for the glory of God?
4) Am I on a quest for thinness to impress others, or do I seek to cultivate eating habits that honor God?
5) Do I exercise to try to create or maintain a "good figure," or do I exercise to strengthen my body for God's service?
6) Is there anything about my appearance that I wish I could change, or am I fully grateful to God for the way he created me?
7) Am I jealous of the appearance of others, or am I truly glad when I observe other women who are more physically attractive than I?
8) Do I covet the wardrobe of others, or do I genuinely rejoice when other women are able to afford and purchase new clothing?

9) When I attend an event or activity, do I sinfully compare myself with others, or do I go asking God to show me whom to love and how to do it?

10) Do I ever dress immodestly or with the intent of drawing attention to myself, or do I always dress in a manner that pleases God?

Asking these questions on a consistent basis can help us weed out worldly values and cultivate a heart for God's priorities.

"TEN LOOKS AT CHRIST"

By God's grace we can put to death the evil desires in our hearts that crave attention from others and that lead us to compare ourselves with others. Colossians 3:1–5 gives us the key to being freed from self-absorption:

> If then you have been raised with Christ, seek the things that are above, where Christ is, seated at the right hand of God. Set your minds on things that are above, not on things that are on earth. For you have died, and your life is hidden with Christ in God. When Christ who is your life appears, then you also will appear with him in glory. Put to death therefore what is earthly in you: sexual immorality, impurity, passion, evil desire, and covetousness, which is idolatry.

Do you see the progression in these verses? Before we are told to put to death "what is earthly" in us, we are told to put our hearts and minds on "things that are above."

The starting point for all repentance is setting our hearts and minds on "what is above." This means to direct our attention toward Jesus Christ and his finished work on the cross. To set our hearts and minds on "what is above" means to intentionally focus on Jesus Christ and to continually remind ourselves that because of his death on the cross, we are forgiven of every evil desire, we are justified from every evil desire, and we are no longer enslaved by any evil desire.

Robert Murray McCheyne had a wonderful antidote to self-focus. He suggested that we should take ten looks at Christ for every look at ourselves. Every time we are tempted to be discouraged by our own disappointing performance, we must look to our Savior, whose perfect performance has been credited to us. Jesus died to redeem us from both the *penalty* and the *power* of sin in our lives. May we revel in his grace and marvel at his mercy in our lives! To set our hearts and minds on the things above means to be taken up with the beauty of his amazing grace and his undeserved mercy in our lives.

PRACTICAL CHANGES

Let's consider some practical changes in our thinking and behavior that we may need to make to develop biblical beauty goals. First, we have to resolve whom we are to trying please in our pursuit of beauty.

Single women, you have only one person to please: the Lord should be the object of your pursuit for beauty (1 Cor. 7:34). All your thoughts, motives, and actions related to beauty should be for the eyes of One and One only.

Married women, we have two to please: God and our husbands. It might sound like heresy to say that we are to consider the opinion of someone besides God, but let me explain. God calls a married woman to please her husband; so therefore you are pleasing God when you seek to please your husband. You need to find out your husband's preferences with regard to how you care for your appearance. How does he want you to dress, style your hair, or wear (or not wear) cosmetics? As a way to reverence your husband, you need to take care of your physical appearance in a way that appeals to him.

Seeking to please the Lord does not mean that we neglect our personal appearance. Pure devotion to God will produce an appropriate concern for physical appearance. A godly woman will seek to present an outward appearance that honors God and attracts others to her character.

It is not wrong to seek to enhance our own appearance, but we need to evaluate our motives and our commitment to modesty. It is not necessarily evil to wear stylish clothing and an attractive hairstyle. It is not sinful to wear makeup and jewelry. The Proverbs 31 woman wore colorful, high-quality clothing. The bride in the Song of Solomon adorned her appearance with jewelry. We are told that Esther underwent twelve months of beauty treatments—six months with oil and myrrh and six with perfumes and cosmetics. The Bible does not condemn wearing and using these things. It is wearing them for the wrong reasons that God's Word forbids.

When the Lord is the object of our desire for beauty, we will have a proper concern about our own physical appearance. As John Piper says in his book *A Godward Life*: "With God at the center—like the 'sun,' satisfying a woman's longing for beauty and greatness and truth and love—all the 'planets' of food and dress and exercise and cosmetics and posture and countenance will stay in their proper orbit."[5]

HIS DESIGN, HIS CLAIM

In the pursuit of true beauty, we each need to acknowledge God's providence and receive with gratefulness the body and appearance he has given to us.

I know this isn't easy. I've always disliked the appearance of my hands. Though I've complained through the years about my thin, fine hair and my knobby knees, I used to be overly concerned about the appearance of my hands. I have very long fingers and veins that pop out no matter what I do. I remember being mortified one day in high school when a girl sitting next to me in orchestra class began scrutinizing my hands. "Your fingers are so long!" she announced loudly as she held up her small hand to mine in comparison. But that wasn't enough. She also required verification from everyone in the class about the extraordinary extra half-inch of fingertip that I possessed. After her comments, my disdain for my hands only grew greater.

Years later, however, the Holy Spirit was kind enough to use a passage of Scripture to correct my attitude toward my hands. I discovered Proverbs 31 where the woman of virtue is described as working with "eager hands" (v. 13). Also, "she opens her arms to the poor and extends her hands to the needy" (v. 20). The King James Version mentions her hands six times, commending the wisdom of a woman who, by the fruit of her hands, can buy a field and plant a vineyard.

I realized my hands weren't merely decorative—they had a kingdom purpose! I saw how sinful (not to mention silly!) it was to care about the *appearance* of my hands instead of my Creator's *purpose* in making them. God has given me these hands as a means of grace to serve and reach out to others.

A loving God has determined what we each look like. He decided our body shape, how tall we would be, the color of our eyes, and all the unique features that make up our body type and appearance—right down to our fingers! We can either spend our lives pining about the results of God's determination or receive with gratefulness his design, knowing that he does all things for his glory.

David said, "I praise you, for I am fearfully and wonderfully made" (Ps. 139:14). When was the last time you worshiped God for the way he created your body? Anything less than a heart filled with gratitude and praise to God for our physical appearance is sinful and grieves the Lord.

WE BELONG TO ANOTHER

We need to remember that our bodies are not our own. First Corinthians 6 says, "Your body is a temple of the Holy Spirit. . . . You are not your own. . . . So glorify God in your body" (vv. 19–20).

Do you treat your body as if it is not your own, tending to it as if belonged to another? We usually take extra-special care of something that belongs to someone else. Some years ago, after a special event at our church, a kind woman gave me the centerpiece from her table. It was a beautiful flower arrangement that she had created and displayed in a china teapot. She graciously told me to enjoy the flowers and return the teapot at my convenience. I did enjoy that flower arrangement, but you can be sure I took special care of that china teapot! I kept it out of the reach of my little boy, who was three at the time, and I exhorted all my daughters to be especially careful with it. I took special care with this china teapot because it belonged to someone else, and I wanted to return it undamaged.

In the same way, your body is not your own—it belongs to God. Your body is the temple of the Holy Spirit—you house the Holy Spirit in your own body! That should make all the difference in how you treat it. This new understanding of our bodies can change not only what we do, but why we do it.

We need to be disciplined in our exercise not merely to look better, but so we can have more energy to serve God.

We should be self-controlled in what we eat not merely to maintain a certain weight, but because self-control is a fruit of the Spirit.

Knowing we belong to God changes our motive in caring for the body he has given us.

ADORNED IN MODESTY

God's Word provides the standard for how we are to clothe our bodies:

> Women should adorn themselves in respectable apparel, with modesty and self-control, not with braided hair and gold or pearls or costly attire, but with what is proper for women who profess godliness—with good works. (1 Tim. 2:9–10)

Our dress is to be proper, modest, and discreet. Those three criteria can help us evaluate whether our clothing, jewelry, hairstyle, and makeup are within biblical guidelines.

Let's consider the word *modest* for a moment. The word has an interesting meaning in the Greek. It means "shamefacedness" or "shame-fastness." The root idea is a sense of shame. This raises the question, of what are we to be ashamed? The text refers to shame in the sense that we should be ashamed if we ever contribute to a man's lustful thinking by our dress. We should be ashamed if we ever cause a man to stumble by our clothing. I don't think any of us is ignorant of the fact that the more of our bodies we expose, the more temptation that provides for men. We should carry a sense of shame about ever causing such a distraction. As we dress, we need to check the motives of our hearts. We should ask ourselves, why am I dressed this way? Am I trying to draw attention to God or to myself? Am I seeking to glorify God or to impress others?

I know that what's fashionable is often immodest, but regardless of how difficult it may be to find modest clothing, there can be no compromise in this area. In trying to determine if something is modest, it is helpful to involve others, to seek their counsel and wisdom. I know many women who have invited their friends to give specific feedback about their wardrobe. I am especially encouraged when I hear of teenage girls who are committed to this standard!

FROM "CONTENTIOUS" TO "PRINCESS"

Does the pursuit of godly beauty sound like a lot of work? I hope not. There is actually a wonderful hope in being set free from an idolatrous focus on self. Most importantly, unlike the physical beauty associated with youth, true beauty grows more lovely with the passing of time. We should be most beautiful when we are sixty, seventy, and older.

> Do not let your adorning be external—the braiding of hair and the putting on of gold jewelry, or the clothing you wear—but let your adorning be the hidden person of the heart with the imperishable beauty of a gentle and quiet spirit, which in God's sight is very precious. For this is how the holy women who hoped in God used to adorn themselves, by submitting to their own husbands, as Sarah obeyed Abraham, calling him lord. And you are her children, if you do good and do not fear anything that is frightening. (1 Pet. 3:3–6)

This passage informs us that we can actually become more attractive by cultivating "the unfading beauty of a gentle and quiet spirit." This godly beauty will cause others to notice; and if we are married, it will make us attractive to our husbands. Most important, it captures the attention of God himself. It is a mystery how the beauty that we cultivate inwardly can be evident outwardly. But Scripture promises us that the more we adorn our inner self, the lovelier we will become.

Have you ever met a woman who displays this kind of extraordinary beauty, actually growing more attractive the older she gets? Elisabeth Elliot is one such woman in my eyes (though she would be embarrassed to hear me say so). When I met her, she was in her seventies. She is gray-headed, and her skin is wrinkled, as you would expect for a woman her age. Yet she possesses a rare beauty. First Peter 3 provides the explanation. No doubt this woman of God has sought to cultivate "the unfading beauty of a gentle and quiet spirit." I want to have that kind of beauty as I get older.

The apostle Peter describes a woman who had this kind of timeless beauty. He singles out Sarah as one "who obeyed Abraham and called him her master. You are her daughters if you do what is right and do not give way to fear" (1 Pet. 3:6).

I'm glad Peter chose Sarah to be the poster girl for "a gentle and quiet spirit," because that wasn't characteristic of her in her youth. She started life as Sarai, meaning "contentious." That name accurately describes some of the accounts of her life as a younger woman. She displayed jealousy, she was manipulative and cynical, and she was downright mean in the way she treated Hagar. She was hardly the picture of "a gentle and quiet spirit." Yet God is in the name-changing business. He changed the name Sarai to Sarah, which means "princess." At some point Sarah became a woman with that humble and quiet spirit—a woman who hoped in God and was submissive to her husband. Scripture records that Abraham buried her with great mourning and love.

I draw tremendous encouragement from the life of Sarah because there is hope for me and for any believing woman who desires to be truly beautiful in the eyes of the Lord. We can become "princesses" at any age; it's never too late. The reality is that one day my knobby knees will fail, my thin hair will turn completely gray, and my hands will still be long *and* have age spots. These physical features will actually get worse. But if I keep my eyes on the One who is loveliness incarnate, I will grow more beautiful by reflecting him. That is truly valuable, and the Bible says it is of great worth in God's sight. It's a beauty regimen we should all practice.

DADDY'S GIRL:
KNOWING GOD AS FATHER

Mary A. Kassian

See what kind of love the Father has given to us, that we should be called children of God; and so we are. The reason why the world does not know us is that it did not know him.

1 JOHN 3:1

IN THE PAST FEW YEARS, several well-known actresses have announced their intention to bear and raise children alone. Does every child need a father? Increasingly, our society's answer to this question is "no," or at least "not necessarily." A recent piece in *Time* magazine proposed that remaining unmarried can be "incredibly empowering" for women[1]—even when this choice involves raising children without the presence of a father. The article implied that no woman really *needs* a husband and, by extension, that children do not necessarily *need* a father.

Children today become fatherless through promiscuity, abandonment, separation, and divorce in the name of male "freedom" or female "empowerment." The net result is that each night at least 40 percent of American children will go to sleep in homes in which their fathers do not live.[2]

Our society has not only lost the physical presence of fathers, but we have also lost something even more fundamental: We have lost our idea of fatherhood. We are living in a culture of fatherlessness. Unlike earlier periods of father absence caused by war, we now face more than a physical loss affecting some homes. This cultural loss affects every home in one way or another.

Our society is afflicted not only with the absence of fathers, but also with the absence of our *belief* in fathers.[3] Few idea shifts in the last century-plus have had such enormous implications. At stake are who we are as male and female, what type of society we will become, and even more importantly, the way we understand and relate to God.

Many people—inside as well as outside the church—no longer believe in the fatherhood of God. Skeptical, hostile feelings toward men have translated into skeptical, hostile feelings toward the God who relates to his chosen people as father. And yet the need to be well-fathered is a fundamental need of the human heart. It is a need that was put in our spirits by our Creator—the heavenly Father, the true Father—who alone defines what fatherhood means and what fatherhood was meant to be. As we will see, relating to God as father is essential to our spiritual well-being and is central to what it means to be a believer.

GOD WANTS TO RELATE TO YOU AS "FATHER"

God is our Father. That does not mean that God is male. He is spirit. And he encompasses all that is good in masculinity and femininity. The Bible at times uses feminine analogies when speaking of God's actions and attributes: he carried the nation Israel in his womb (Isa. 46:3); he cries out like a woman in labor (Isa. 42:14); he birthed the Jewish nation (Deut. 32:18); he has compassion on us as a mother has compassion for the baby at her breast (Isa. 49:15); he nurses and nurtures us (Ps. 131:2); he comforts as a mother comforts (Isa. 66:13). These and other passages exhibit the beautiful, tender, "feminine," nurturing aspect of God's character.

Because of these mother-like analogies, many in the Christian community minimize or even deny the importance of the name "Father" for God. They argue that it is but one name among many and claim that, given the times in which we live, we ought not to regard it as his preferred name. They suggest that we call him "Mother," "Mother and Father," or "Heavenly Parent" or use non-gender-specific names such as "Source" or "Creator." Many women, particularly those who come into Christianity from non-religious backgrounds, wrestle with the idea of addressing God with masculine pronouns.

WHY DO WE CALL GOD "FATHER"?

This is a question that demands an articulate biblical answer—particularly in this day and age. The first and most obvious reason we call him "Father" is that this is what he wants to be called. The first person of the Trinity has many names—Almighty One, Creator, Most High, Holy Holy Holy, the Rock, the Great I Am. But when Jesus came to tear away the veil so we could look directly into the heart of God, he revealed God as "Father." Jesus used "Father" more than any other description or name for God. And he taught us to address God in the same way: "Our Father who art in heaven . . . " *Father* is God's self-revealed designation.

What do you think of when you hear the word *father*? I think of sitting perched on the splintery counter of my carpenter dad's dusty workshop, watching him work. I think of the pungent smell of freshly cut wood. I think of his huge, strong, callused hands. I think of learning my multiplication tables by pounding groups of nails into a two-by-four. I think of the white doll cradle he built for my sixth birthday, the set of bedroom furniture he built for my twelfth birthday, the basement renovation he helped me with last year. I think of being rescued in snowstorms. Watching fireworks from the roof. Folding paper stars at Christmas. Being tickled until my sides hurt.

Many women do not have good thoughts and feelings when they hear the word *father*. To them, the word means abandonment, anger, shame, insecurity, fear, unpredictability, conflict, or pain. But whether your thoughts are good or bad, it is undeniable that the word means something to you. That is because *father* is a word that has a specific meaning. The concept is not abstract. When you speak of your father, I know you are speaking of a person who has profoundly affected your life. I know you are speaking of someone who is or was alive—someone who has individual characteristics and a distinct personality—someone with whom you might interact and relate. Whether positive or negative, the word *father* means something very real to each of us. We all have a strong, clear concept of what *father* means—or what it ought to mean.

It is astounding that God wants us to call him Father. The implications are staggering. Having God as our Father means that he is a living, personal being and not an impersonal force. It means we can get to know him. It means we can talk to him and interact with him. It means we can relate to him on a personal and even an intimate basis. I might not know how to relate to an Almighty One, a Most High, or the Great I Am, because I have not met anybody like that. I have no earthly frame of reference to do so. But relating to a father? That's different. *Father* does not denote an abstract force, a metaphysical power, or a cosmic aura. It speaks of a person with a distinct personality and characteristics. I believe that God would have us call him "Father" because it is a personal term that refers to a personal being with whom we can personally relate.

Father is also the term that best describes God's relationships—who he is in relationship to others. God relates to his Son, Jesus, and to us, his adopted children, as Father. *Father* implies family interaction. It implies causality and dependency, for a father is the source of life. It implies love and intimacy. It implies certain roles and responsibilities. Father is the pacesetter. He is the initiator, visionary, boundary-setter, source, and final authority in the home. A good father is committed to his family. He loves, protects, and provides. He lovingly guides, corrects, and teaches his children. A father also bequeaths an inheritance upon his children.

Consider the Father God's relationship with his son, Jesus. The Father has greater authority than Christ (John 13:16; 14:28; 17:2). Though equal in essence, Jesus submits himself to the Father's will (Phil. 2:6–8). It was the Father who sent Jesus to secure redemption on our behalf (John 3:16–17; 17:3). Jesus always does what pleases his Father (John 8:29). Jesus follows his Father's directives exactly (John 14:31). He learns from his Father (John 15:15), speaks his Father's words (John 8:28; 14:24; 17:8), does his Father's work (John 10:25; 14:10), and brings glory to his Father (John 14:13). The Father highly exalted his Son (Phil. 2:9; Heb. 5:7–10) and appointed him "heir of all things" (Heb. 1:2). Jesus is the rightful heir to everything that belongs to his Father (John 16:15). Everything that Jesus has comes from him (John 17:7, 22, 24).

The word *father* denotes a different type of relationship than the word *mother, brother, sister, aunt,* or *uncle.* It is the term that most accurately represents the nature of the relationship between the first and second persons of the Trinity. And it is the term that most accurately represents the nature of God's relationship to us. God calls himself "Father" because the word characterizes his relationships better than any other word.

"Father" is the most significant name of the God of the Bible. It is the name that sets Christianity apart from all the other religions of the world. Other religions invite us to worship their gods, allahs, creators, or metaphysical forces, but Christianity invites us to believe in a Son and to enter into an intimate family relationship with a loving Father. Jesus, the Son of God, came so that we could meet his Father, be adopted into the family of God, and relate to the almighty God of the universe in an intimate, personal, concrete way as sons and daughters. As God said, "I will make my dwelling among them and walk among them, and I will be their God, and they shall be my people. . . . I will be a father to you, and you shall be sons and daughters to me" (2 Cor. 6:16, 18).

If we do not know and relate to God as Father, then we do not really understand the gospel. As theologian J. I. Packer said in his classic book *Knowing God*:

> You sum up the whole of New Testament teaching in a single phrase, if you speak of it as a revelation of the Fatherhood of the holy Creator. In the same way, you sum up the whole of New Testament religion if you describe it as the knowledge of God as one's holy Father. If you want to judge how well a person understands Christianity, find out how much he makes of the thought of being God's child, and having God as his Father. If this is not the thought that prompts and controls his worship and prayers and his whole outlook on life, it means that he does not understand Christianity very well at all. For everything that Christ taught, everything that makes the New Testament new, and better than the Old, everything that is distinctively Christian as opposed to merely Jewish, is summed up in the knowledge of the Fatherhood of God. "Father" is the Christian name for God.[4]

Father is the Christian name for God. God is not merely like a father as he is like a rock, like a fortress, like a shepherd, or like a warrior. God is Father, and he alone defines what true fatherhood means. How tragic and foolish and how very arrogant of us to shy away from this name because some human males are poor examples of fatherhood or because our culture regards a God named "Father" as oppressive and patriarchal.

JESUS POINTS US TO THE FATHER-HEART OF GOD

When Jesus was on earth, his whole message was "come meet my Dad!" "Look at me," he said, "and see what my Father is like. See how I imitate him! Let me tell you how much my Father loves me! The love I have for you reveals how much my Father loves you! The miracles I do are a result of the compassion and power of my Father! The words I say—the things I teach—this truth comes from my Father! Listen to me talk to my Father. Watch me spend time with my Father. Through me, he can be your Father too!"

Jesus points us to the Father-heart of God. In one of Christ's final prayers before his crucifixion, he reported to his Father, "I made known to them your name, and I will continue to make it known, that the love with which you have loved me may be in them, and I in them" (John 17:26). Jesus makes known who the Father is and what the Father does. He informed Philip, who was asking to see the Father, "Whoever has seen me has seen the Father" (John 14:9). Jesus claimed that when we look at him, we see the One who sent him (John 12:45). Jesus revealed the Father to us. He is "the exact imprint of his nature" (Heb. 1:3).

Jesus shows us what the fatherhood of God is like. He demonstrates the mercy of the Father, the Father's gentleness, the Father's patience, the Father's power, the Father's passion, and the Father's overwhelming love. And he leads us to the Father. Consider what he said in John 14:6—"I am the way. . . . No one comes to the Father except through me." Jesus is not our destination; Jesus is "the way"— the portal. He is the way to the Father's heart. When we come to Christ, we are ushered into the Father's presence.

According to Jesus, knowing the Father and Son is the essence of what it means to have eternal life. Jesus said, "This is eternal life, that they know you the only true God, and Jesus Christ whom you have sent" (John 17:3). Jesus was consumed with thoughts of the Father. His relationship with the Father permeated everything he said and everything he did. And he came so we could be adopted into the same sort of a child-father relationship. This was his whole purpose, his whole mission. Securing the right for us to be reconciled to the Father was the reason for the cross.

What does it mean to be in a relationship with the Father? First John 1:3 says, "Our fellowship is with the Father and with his Son Jesus Christ." Have you ever paused to consider what this means? The Greek word for *fellowship* is *koinonia*. *Koinonia* means "sharing," "connecting," "communicating." Being in a relationship with the Father means that we share, connect, and communicate with him. According to Christ's prayer in John 17, it means that we know the Father and experience his love. Knowing him is a process of becoming increasingly familiar with his character and his ways; it means a growing capacity to recognize his voice, his face, his hand, and his heart.

Jesus taught that his Father loves us just as much he loves his Son (John 17:23). He prayed that the mighty love that the Father has for him would also be in us. Can you imagine? If you are in a relationship with God, the immense, full force of the Father's love for his Son is directed toward *you*!

How well do you know the Father? Are you going ever deeper in your relationship with him? Are you confidently and joyfully entering into the Father's presence? Do you experience his love for you as his daughter?

GOD HAS PUT A FATHER-LONGING IN YOUR HEART

A number of years ago, in a small town in Spain, there was a young man named Juan. Juan was wild and rebellious. His father's attempts to correct him had failed. At one point Juan stole a large sum of money from his father and ran away from home.

Month after month there was no word of him. The father loved his son and wanted him to come home. So when he heard that someone had seen Juan in the city, he went to search for him. The father drove up and down the streets, showed Juan's picture to strangers, and checked in bars, but to no avail. Finding his son in such a large city was surely an impossible task.

Finally an idea struck him. He took out an ad in the local paper. It read: "Juan: All is forgiven. I long to see you again. Please meet me on Saturday at noon on the steps of City Hall. Love, Dad."

When Saturday came and the father went to the appointed place, he found, along with his son, more than a hundred other boys named Juan sitting on the steps of City Hall. All the boys were longing—yearning—to have a relationship with the fathers from whom they were estranged.

There is something within each one of us that yearns for a relationship with a good father. Several years ago singer/songwriter Bob Carlisle wrote a ballad entitled "Butterfly Kisses." The song spoke of the tender love between a father and his daughter. It quickly climbed to the top of the charts and received international recognition. In reflecting upon the song's enormous success, Carlisle said, "I get a lot of mail from young girls who try to get me to marry their moms. That used to be a real chuckle because it's so cute, but then I realized they don't want a romance for Mom. They want the father that is in that song, and that just kills me."[5]

Those girls want the dad that is in the song. They want a dad to love them, protect them, and be kind and tender toward them. They want a dad who is strong, dependable, and unswerving in his commitment to his family—someone to help them, mentor them, and be their biggest fan. They want this dad so much that they write to a perfect stranger whose only contact with them has been through a song played on the radio about his love for his own daughter, begging him to marry their mom so they can have the father of their dreams.

The human need for being fathered is deep. And the longing expressed by these little girls and by all the Juans that showed up on the steps of City Hall is reminiscent of the longing for the Father God that resides in each of our hearts. Our spirits long to be fathered by the father of our dreams—our perfect heavenly Father.

When we become Christians, we are adopted into a family relationship. In ancient Roman culture, the process of adoption involved several carefully prescribed legal procedures. First, a father chose the child he wanted to adopt. Then the child's legal and social relationships to his natural family were severed. All his previous debts and obligations were eradicated, as if they had never existed. The child was then placed permanently into his new family and was endowed with the same prestige and privilege as a natural child, including that of being an heir. Multiple witnesses sealed the process.[6] Our adoption process is similar.

Our heavenly Father chooses us to be adopted into his family. He severs the legal and social ties we have to sin. In grace, through Christ, he frees us from all our debts and obligations. He places us in the family of God and endows us with prestige, privilege, and inheritance. The Holy Spirit is proof of the adoption.

The Holy Spirit is also called "the Spirit of his Son" (Gal. 4:6), "the Spirit of adoption" (Rom. 8:15), and "the Spirit of your Father" (Matt. 10:20). It is this Spirit—the Spirit of Sonship, the Spirit of Adoption, and the Spirit of the Father—who lives in my heart and in yours. And it is this Spirit who calls and drives us to intimacy with the Father, causing us to cry out: "Abba!" *Abba* is an informal Aramaic term for Father, indicating tenderness, intimacy, affection, and dependency.[7] It is the cry of a child calling out for "Daddy."

> And because you are sons, God has sent the Spirit of his Son into your hearts, crying, "Abba! Father!" (Gal. 4:6)

> For you did not receive the spirit of slavery to fall back into fear, but you have received the Spirit of adoption as sons, by whom we cry, "Abba! Father!" The Spirit himself bears witness with our spirit that we are children of God. (Rom. 8:15–16)

Did you notice the first phrase of Romans 8:15: "For you did not receive the spirit of slavery to fall back into fear"? Some of you are so afraid of your Father God. You are afraid that Father God is going to abandon you—or belittle, disappoint, hurt, or yell at you—like your earthly father did. That is not the Holy Spirit in you talking. The Holy Spirit is not "the spirit of slavery . . . into fear." The Holy Spirit in your heart cries out, "Abba! Father!"

The word *cry* in the Romans text indicates a spontaneous expression of intensity, full of emotional depth and longing. It is used in its present tense. Literally, "Your spirit is *even now* crying out Abba!" It speaks of the unrestrained heart-cry of those controlled by the Spirit of God. Under the influence of the Spirit, our whole being—heart, mind, soul, and strength—cries out with intense longing to connect with the Father. It is a strong, intense, desperate, felt need that calls us and drives us to the Father's heart.

Do you wonder why you feel no peace in your heart? Do you wonder why you feel restless and unsettled? Do you wonder why you feel frustrated? Perhaps it is because the Holy Spirit in you is crying "Daddy! Daddy! Daddy!" But you are busy, occupied with other things. Or you are too afraid to look into the Father's eyes and let him love you.

YOUR HEART-LONGING WILL ONLY BE SATISFIED IN A LOVE RELATIONSHIP WITH HIM

Christianity is a love relationship with the Father and Son. It is God's loving me and me loving him back. The Father lavishes his children with love. The apostle John exclaimed: "See what kind of love the Father has given to us, that we should be called children of God" (1 John 3:1). To lavish means to give freely and profusely. The word indicates an exceedingly liberal, abundant, and extravagant outpouring.

Do you find it difficult to accept the fact that the Father loves you? Not just to know it in your head but to really believe it deep in your heart? Do you believe that the Father wants to relate to you on a personal basis—that he wants to be close to you and have an intimate relationship with you? Do you believe that he delights in you and wants to spend time with you? At the root of much of our depression, our self-loathing, and our hopelessness and despair is the faulty belief that God could not possibly love us.

Do you know that the Father knows your name? He says, "I will go before you and level the exalted places. . . . I will give you the . . . hoards in secret places. . . . I call you by your name" (Isa. 45:2–4).

Do you know that he keeps track of the most minute details of your life—including the number of cells in your body and the number of hairs on your head? "Even the hairs of your head are all numbered" (Matt. 10:30).

Do you know that the Father collects your tears in his bottle? "You have kept count of my tossings; put my tears in your bottle. Are they not in your book?" (Ps. 56:8).

Do you know that he has inscribed you on the palm of his hand? "Behold, I have engraved you on the palms of my hands; your walls are continually before me" (Isa. 49:16).

Do you know that his heart is stirred and aroused with compassion when he thinks of you? "As a father shows compassion to his children, so the LORD shows compassion to those who fear him" (Ps. 103:13).

Do you know that he has his cord of love tethered to your heart and is gently drawing you closer? "When Israel was a child, I loved him, and out of Egypt I called my son. . . . It was I who taught Ephraim to walk; I took them up by their arms, but they did not know that I healed them. I led them with cords of kindness, with the bands of love, and I became to them as one who eases the yoke on their jaws, and I bent down to them and fed them" (Hos. 11:1, 3–4).

What an astounding picture of the Father's heart. His is a mighty, mighty love. The Father loves you and wants a love relationship with you. He wants your heart. He says, "How I would set you among my sons, and give you a pleasant land, a heritage most beautiful of all nations. And I thought you would call me, My Father, and would not turn from following me" (Jer. 3:19).

The Father appreciates your obedience. He appreciates your disciplines of prayer and fasting and being in the Word. He appreciates your service. But more than all these things and at the center of the gospel is this: the Father wants your heart. He does not want rote obedience, conformity, service, sacrifice, and ceaseless ministry from you. If he does not have your heart, these things mean nothing to him. Living in a love relationship with God is the key to enjoying and delighting in him and experiencing his delight in you. If you truly understand this and take it to heart, it will revolutionize your life and will allow you to begin to experience the joy and victory that Christ has already won for you.

Understanding Christianity as a love relationship revolutionizes the way we live. It changes the way we view repentance and confession. We repent and confess because we have hurt the one we love, not merely because we have broken the rules. It changes the way we view witnessing. We witness because we want people to get to know our wonderful Brother and Father, not to convert them to a church or religion. It changes our perspective on Christian disciplines. We read the Bible, pray, memorize, meditate, and fast not because it is required of us, but because of our longing to connect with the lover and redeemer of our souls. We are motivated by love and longing, not duty and obligation. It changes our perspective on Christian service.

We are under no pressure to perform. We listen carefully to our Father and do only what he asks of us. We delight in our Father and revel in being his child. It changes our perspective on suffering, pain, and sacrifice. We are filled with joy and hope in the certainty that our Father is in control and will make it right. We are eager to give up lesser joys for the all-surpassing joy of knowing and walking with him.

Are you living your life in a love relationship with your Abba-Father? Are you nurturing or neglecting that relationship? Are you running toward or away from him?

Just across the street from the house where I grew up in Canada is a ravine that flows toward the deep valley of Edmonton's North Saskatchewan River. In the winter, when it freezes to a depth of a couple of feet, the ravine is safe to walk and skate on. But in the spring the ice melts from the bottom up, and it is difficult to tell how much has melted underneath. Because of this, children are warned to stay off the ice in the spring.

One spring, despite repeated warnings, an eleven-year-old boy, Jordan, his eleven-year-old friend Bryce (not their real names), and Bryce's six-year-old brother clambered down through the dense thickets and poplars to play in a culvert beneath a century-old wooden trestle. The boys had taken only a few steps inside the culvert when the ice suddenly cracked, sending Jordan and the six-year-old tumbling into the chilly water. Bryce pulled out his young brother and then ran for a branch to extend to his friend. Seconds later, when Bryce returned, Jordan was gone, swept under the ice by the swift current of the spring waters. Horror-stricken and terrified, Bryce and his brother told no one. It was not until police questioned Jordan's classmates at school the next day that Bryce broke down and confessed.

Firemen and policemen used chain saws, augers, and picks to break through the ice below the culvert. Commercial divers probed the murky spring meltwater. The task was extremely dangerous. The ice, which ranged in thickness from eight inches to five feet, was unstable. The water was frigid and could quickly cause hypothermia. Furthermore, the task was extremely tedious. Jordan's body might have been trapped anywhere between the culvert and the place where the ravine spilled into the river—two miles downstream. Late that afternoon the search was officially postponed until the ice thawed. But that wasn't good enough for Jordan's father.

The following morning his father returned with rented chainsaws and augers and broke through the ice in various spots, slowly working his way down the winding creek. With mirrors and flashlights he peered into air pockets between the ice and flowing water, hoping to catch a glimpse of his son. Wearing hip waders, he chipped away at the ice day after day, often with numb and bloodied hands. News of his dogged persistence aroused the compassion of the city, and dozens of complete strangers came out to help. Day after day, dawn till dusk, the search continued. A week after the drowning, it was starting to look hopeless. Most of the helpers had given up. But though he showed signs of exhaustion, the father refused to stop looking. In an interview he explained, "I can't rest until I find him."

On the eighth day, a spectator spotted Jordan's body jammed beneath a thick shelf of ice. A hush fell as his father waded into the creek, pulled his son's cold, stiff body from the water, and wept.

Like Jordan's father, our heavenly Father looks for us when we run away. He does not rest. He does not give up when all others have lost hope. Day after day he persists until he holds his wayward child in his arms. But unlike Jordan's father, our heavenly Father can bend over and breathe life into our stiff, frozen souls. He breathes again and again until our cheeks turn from blue to white to pink. He holds us close to his heart until our heart pumps blood and our limbs begin to move again.

Consider your relationship to your heavenly Father. Are you neglectful of him, playing by the side of the creek, unaware of the danger of the ice? Have you fallen into the chilling water? Are you being swept away in the current? Do you feel cold and numb? Are you aware of your need for him to hold you and breathe life into your spirit? Do you know and love your Father?

In the last verse of the Old Testament, the prophet Malachi looked forward to a time when the hearts of the fathers would turn to the children and the hearts of the children to their fathers. Even now, our heavenly Father's heart is turned toward you. Will you turn your heart toward him?

PART TWO

The Challenge of Biblical Womanhood in a Fallen World

PORTRAIT OF A WOMAN
USED BY GOD

Nancy Leigh DeMoss

WHAT DOES A "GODLY WOMAN" LOOK LIKE? How can our lives fulfill the eternal purpose for which God created us? How can we bear "much fruit" (John 15:5) for his glory? Thankfully, the Word of God gives us the instruction we need; it also provides a number of role models—women who illustrate what it means to walk with God and to be used by him.

Though these women lived in settings quite different from our own, they faced many of the same challenges we face: they were daughters and wives and mothers; they experienced youth, adulthood, and old age; they had to wrestle with the mysteries of life and death, faith and doubt, joy and sorrow. As we study their portraits, we are instructed in the ways of God and find a pattern for our own lives.

One of my favorite biblical role models is Mary of Nazareth. In her life I have found a wealth of wisdom for my own walk with God. Her story illustrates many of the characteristics of the kind of woman God uses to fulfill his redemptive purposes in our world.

The Gospel of Luke records that dramatic moment in which Mary first became aware that God had an extraordinary purpose for her life. As the account unfolds, we are given a glimpse into the heart and character of this remarkable woman of God.

In the sixth month the angel Gabriel was sent from God to a city of Galilee named Nazareth, to a virgin betrothed to a man whose name was Joseph, of the house of David. And the virgin's name was Mary. And he came to her and said, "Greetings, O favored one, the Lord is with you!" But she was greatly troubled at the saying, and tried to discern what sort of greeting this might be. And the angel said to her, "Do not be afraid, Mary, for you have found favor with God. And behold, you will conceive in your womb and bear a son, and you shall call his name Jesus. He will be great and will be called the Son of the Most High. And the Lord God will give to him the throne of his father David, and he will reign over the house of Jacob forever, and of his kingdom there will be no end."

And Mary said to the angel, "How will this be, since I am a virgin?"

And the angel answered her, "The Holy Spirit will come upon you, and the power of the Most High will overshadow you; therefore the child to be born will be called holy—the Son of God. And behold, your relative Elizabeth in her old age has also conceived a son, and this is the sixth month with her who was called barren. For nothing will be impossible with God." And Mary said, "Behold, I am the servant of the Lord; let it be to me according to your word." And the angel departed from her. (Luke 1:26–38)

MARY WAS AN ORDINARY WOMAN

There was nothing particularly unusual about Mary. She was not from a wealthy or illustrious family. When the angel appeared to this young teenage girl, she was engaged to be married and was undoubtedly doing what engaged girls do—dreaming of being married to Joseph, of the home they would live in, of the family they would have. I don't believe she was expecting her life to be used in any extraordinary way.

The significance of Mary's life was not based on any of the things our world values so highly—background, physical beauty, intelligence, education, natural gifts and abilities. It was Mary's relationship to Jesus that gave her life significance. We would not be reading this account today if it were not for the fact that she was related to Jesus. "The Lord is with you," the angel said. That is what made all the difference in this young woman's life. And it is what makes all the difference in our lives.

Don't assume you have to be extraordinary to be used by God. You don't have to have exceptional gifts, talents, abilities, or connections. God specializes in using ordinary people whose limitations and weaknesses make them ideal showcases for his greatness and glory:

> For consider your calling, brothers: not many of you were wise according to worldly standards, not many were powerful, not many were of noble birth. But God chose what is foolish in the world to shame the wise; God chose what is weak in the world to shame the strong; God chose what is low and despised in the world . . . so that no human being might boast in the presence of God. (1 Cor. 1:26–29)

Regardless of how ordinary and "unqualified" we may be, all of us as children of God can walk with him and be used by him—not because we are inherently significant, but because of our relationship with Christ. Our true identity is not found in a job, a mate, a child, a position, or a possession. It is our connection to the Lord Jesus Christ that gives our lives value and significance and makes us usable in his kingdom.

MARY WAS A PURE WOMAN

Though she had grown up in a community renowned for moral corruption, she was a virgin. Undoubtedly, many of Mary's peers had not kept themselves pure. But when God was ready to send his Son into the world to bring about his eternal plan of redemption, he chose to place the seed of his Son into the womb of a pure vessel. He selected a woman who had not given in to the lure of the world but had kept herself for the Master's use.

In a world that flaunts perversion and scoffs at purity, women of God must be willing to go against the flow—to walk in purity and to teach their daughters the importance and value of a commitment to personal and moral virtue.

You may be reaping the blessings and benefits of a lifelong commitment to personal purity. On the other hand, you may be living with a deep sense of loss and regret from having made wrong choices. Perhaps you feel that God will never be able to use you because you have not kept yourself pure. The wonder of God's grace is that he can and he will restore purity to those who come to him in contrition and true repentance. He cannot restore the virginity you sacrificed, but by his grace he can restore true virtue.

MARY WAS AN UNDESERVING WOMAN

God did not choose this young woman because she was worthy of the honor of being the mother of the Savior. The angel said to Mary, "Greetings, O *favored one!*" (v. 28). That phrase could be translated, ". . . you who are graciously accepted." If any of us is to be accepted by God, it will be because of grace—not because of anything we have done.

> *Nothing in my hand I bring,*
> *Simply to Thy cross I cling;*
> *Naked, come to Thee for dress;*
> *Helpless, look to Thee for grace.*
> —AUGUSTUS TOPLADY, "ROCK OF AGES"

It's all because of grace. Over and over again in Scripture, we see that God chooses people who are undeserving. God didn't look down from heaven and say, "I see a woman who has something to offer me; I think I'll use her." Mary did not deserve to be used by God; to the contrary, she marveled at God's grace in choosing her.

The moment we cease to see ourselves as undeserving instruments, chances are we will cease to be useful in the hand of God.

MARY WAS A CHOSEN WOMAN

She was chosen by God for a task of eternal significance—to bear the life of the Son of God. There is a sense in which God has chosen all of us for a similar task—to bring forth spiritual life. "You did not choose me, but I chose you and appointed you that you should go and bear fruit and that your fruit should abide" (John 15:16).

I believe there is a special sense in which God created us as women to be bearers and nurturers of life. Whether or not he grants us physical children, he wants to use us to carry the life and light of Jesus into the world—to be spiritual reproducers, bringing forth his life in the lives of others.

We may look at certain prominent or unusually gifted people and think they have been uniquely chosen by God. The fact is, if you are a child of God, *you* have been chosen by God for a task of supreme significance—to be a bearer and nurturer of spiritual life by carrying the life of the Lord Jesus to others.

Once you look at your life that way, you'll never again have a "self-image" problem. Many women today carry scars of rejection from parents, mates, or friends who have spurned them. What a joy to discover that though we deserve to be rejected by God, we have been chosen to belong to him and to be a part of his redemptive plan in the universe.

MARY WAS A SPIRIT-FILLED WOMAN

We too must be filled with the Spirit if we are to fulfill the purpose for which God has chosen us. When the angel said to Mary, "You will conceive in your womb and bear a son," Mary responded, "How will this be, since I am a virgin?" God had chosen her for a task that was humanly impossible.

The task for which God has chosen you and me is no less impossible. We can share the gospel of Christ with our lost friends, but we cannot give them repentance and faith. You can provide a climate that is conducive to the spiritual growth of your children, but you can't make them have a heart for God. We are totally dependent on him to produce any fruit of eternal value.

In response to Mary's expression of weakness and inadequacy, the angel promised her God's strength and adequacy: "The Holy Spirit will come upon you, and the power of the Most High will overshadow you" (v. 35). In the Old Testament *El Elyon* was God Most High, the Creator of heaven and earth.

I can't begin to count how many conversations I've had with the Lord that sound a bit like Mary's exchange with the angel. The Lord gives me a task, and I respond, "Lord, how can this be? I can't do this. There are other people far more qualified. I'm not prepared. I'm not ready. I'm so tired. I'm so weak. I don't know what I'm doing." He responds simply, "I know. That's why I've given you the Holy Spirit. The Holy Spirit will enable you, and my power will overshadow you and your weakness."

Don't ever forget that you cannot do what God has called you to do. You cannot parent that child, love that husband, care for that elderly parent, submit to that boss, teach that Sunday school class, or lead that small-group Bible study.

God specializes in the impossible, so that when the victory is won and the task is complete, we cannot take any credit. Others know we didn't do it, and we know we didn't do it. We must always remember that we can live the Christian life and serve God only through the power of his Holy Spirit. As soon as we think we can handle it on our own, we become useless to him. We have to be willing to get out of the way, let God take over, and let him overshadow us.

MARY WAS AN AVAILABLE WOMAN

Equipped with the promises of God, Mary's response was simply, "I am the servant of the Lord; let it be to me according to your word" (v. 38). In other words, "Lord, I'm available. You are my Master; I am your servant. I'm willing to be used however you choose. My body is yours; my womb is yours; my life is yours."

In that act of surrender, Mary offered herself to God as a living sacrifice. She was willing to be used by God for his purposes—willing to endure the loss of reputation that was certain to follow when people realized she was with child, willing to endure the ridicule and even the possible stoning permitted by the Mosaic law, willing to go through nine months of increasing discomfort and sleeplessness, willing to endure the labor pains of giving birth to the Child. Mary was willing to give up her own plans and agenda so that she might link arms with God in fulfilling his agenda.

That was the heart attitude of a young woman named Betty Stam, who along with her husband, John, went to China as a missionary. In 1934, at the ages of twenty-seven and twenty-eight, they were martyred at the hands of the Communists. The following prayer, written nine years earlier, explains why she was willing to make this ultimate sacrifice:

> Lord, I give up my own purposes and plans, all my own desires and hopes and ambitions . . . and accept Thy will for my life. I give myself, my life, my all, utterly to Thee, to be Thine forever. . . . Work out Thy whole will in my life, at any cost, now and forever.[1]

This ought to be the heart-cry of every woman of God. "I am your servant; I'm available. Do you want me to be married? I'll be married. Do you want me to be single? I'll be single. Do you want me to have children? I'll raise children for your glory. Do you want me to be child-less? Then I will be a reproducer of spiritual fruit in the lives of others. Do you want me to live in a small, overcrowded house? Do you want me to suffer with a physical affliction? Do you want me to homeschool my children? Do you want me to love and serve this husband who is so hard to live with? Do you want me to take that young woman under my wing and mentor her in your ways? Do you want me to give up my free time to tutor that child from a broken home? Do you want me to take meals to that cranky neighbor who is ill? Lord, whatever! I am your servant. May it be to me as you have said."

MARY WAS A BELIEVING WOMAN

Following her encounter with the angel, Mary went to visit her cousin Elizabeth. Elizabeth recognized in the younger woman a response of faith to the word of God: "Blessed is she who believed that there would be a fulfillment of what was spoken to her from the Lord" (v. 45). Mary took God at his word. She exercised faith in his ability to fulfill his promise. It was that faith in God and his Word that activated the power and blessing of God in her life. As a result, God fulfilled his promise and a Savior was born.

Years ago Dr. Adrian Rogers challenged a large gathering with these words: "We have no right to be believed so long as we can be explained."[2] Most of our lives are so very explainable because we are relying on natural, human efforts and energy, abilities and plans, programs and methods. What would happen if God's people believed his promises and laid hold on him in prayer, believing him for the impossible—for reconciliation of broken marriages, for the salva-tion of unbelieving friends and relatives, for spiritual transformation of wayward children, for a fresh outpouring of his Spirit in genuine revival? We might see God release from heaven the greatest awaken-ing our world has ever known.

MARY WAS A PRAISING WOMAN

When God puts challenging circumstances in our lives, we either *wor-ship* or we *whine*. I'm ashamed to say I've done more than my share of whining—even about ministry. "Oh, Lord, I'm tired of traveling.

Do I have to go there? This is so hard! Why do I have to deal with that person?" I am reminded of the children of Israel in the wilderness who murmured incessantly. "If only God had just let us die in the wilderness," they whined. One day God finally said in essence, "You want to die in the wilderness? Okay, you'll die in the wilderness!" (see Num. 14:2, 28–30). Be careful what you say when you murmur—God may take you up on it.

But when Mary's world was turned topsy-turvy, when she was faced with a drastic change in plans, she responded in worship and praise. "My soul magnifies the Lord, and my spirit rejoices in God my Savior" (vv. 46–47). So begins her *Magnificat*—one of the greatest hymns of praise ever lifted up to heaven. She worshiped God for his wonderful acts, for his mercy, and for choosing her to be a part of his great redemptive plan.

MARY WAS A WOMAN OF THE WORD

Her prayer in Luke 1:46–55 includes at least a dozen quotations from the Old Testament Scriptures. In those days women did not have a formal education; Mary was probably illiterate. But she had listened to the reading of the Word and had hidden it in her heart. Her life and her prayers were filled with Scripture.

One of our greatest needs as women is to become women of the Word so that our prayers, our responses, and our words are saturated with God's way of thinking. The world does not need to hear our opinions. When friends approach us for advice about dealing with their children, their boss, their finances, their fears, their depression, or other issues, they don't need to hear what we think. We should be able to take them to the Word and say, "I don't have the answers you need, but I know Someone who does. Here's what God's Word has to say about this situation."

God didn't intend for pastors to be the only ones who point people to the Word. Each of us should be able to use the Word effectively, not only in our worship and our own walk, but also in ministering to the needs of others. If we're going to be women of the Word, we must make a priority of spending time daily in the Scripture—reading, studying, memorizing, meditating, personalizing, and praying it back to God—letting him teach us his ways.

MARY WAS A REFLECTIVE WOMAN

Following the birth of the Lord Jesus, we are told that "Mary treasured up all these things, pondering them in her heart" (Luke 2:19). Twelve years later, after Mary and Joseph found Jesus talking with the teachers in the temple, once again we find that she "treasured up all these things in her heart" (v. 51). The two different Greek words translated "treasured" both mean "to keep carefully; to preserve, keep safe, keep close."[3] In the midst of the many responsibilities of being a wife and a mother, Mary took time to contemplate what was happening in her life and to meditate on what God had done.

The hurried, hectic, harried pace of our culture can be addictive and intoxicating. Many of us find ourselves giving in to the temptation to fill every waking moment of our lives with noise and activity. We get in the car and turn on the radio; we walk in the house and turn on the television or the computer or pick up the phone. E-mail, voice mail, cell phones, music, and mass media threaten to fill every bit of available space and to leave us emotionally and spiritually empty and shallow.

If we are going to be instruments of his grace who reflect his light into the darkness around us, we must take time to be quiet—to be still—to ponder and reflect on who God is and what he is doing around and in us.

MARY WAS A HUMBLE WOMAN

Very little is said of this woman after the birth of Jesus. Apparently she was content to be identified as Jesus' mother. She was satisfied to be in the background, not well-known herself, but making him known. The angelic messenger had said of her son, "*He* will be great (Luke 1:32).

Mary did not see herself as worthy of God's favor: "He has looked on the humble estate of his servant" (v. 48). In other words, "Who am I that he should look upon me with favor?" She had the spirit of John the Baptist who said, "He must increase, but I must decrease" (John 3:30). Here was a woman who realized, "It's not about me; it's all about him."

Women today don't always get a lot of strokes for being wives and moms, for faithfully loving and caring for their husbands and children. There is enormous pressure to "*do* something worthwhile," to have our own identity. Even apart from the pressure of the culture, our own hearts long for recognition and appreciation for the sacrifices we make. The woman God uses is a humble woman; she follows in the steps of the Lord Jesus who "made himself nothing, taking the form of a servant" (Phil. 2:7).

MARY WAS A TRUSTING WOMAN

She trusted that God was bigger and greater than her circumstances. Her trusting heart is seen in the first chapter of Matthew, after her life-changing encounter with the angel. Joseph, her betrothed husband, had not seen or heard the angel. When Mary explained what had happened, apparently he didn't believe her. But Mary knew how to trust God and was willing to wait for him to act. She did not push her husband to believe what she knew God had said; rather, she gave God time to speak to her husband and to work in his heart.

Sometimes we as women are sensitive to perceive spiritual truth or insight before the men in our lives do. The natural tendency at that point is to think we have to convince them of the rightness or the importance of the insight we have received.

Mary didn't have that spirit. She didn't try to prove anything. She didn't feel it was her responsibility to convince Joseph. She didn't manipulate or control. She simply waited on the Lord and trusted him to fulfill his purposes. And in his time God sent an angel to reveal to Joseph what he needed to know.

You may be tired of waiting for God to speak to your husband— or your pastor or another spiritual authority. Don't try to take matters into your own hands. Wait on the Lord. Trust him. He will accomplish his purposes in his time and in his way.

MARY WAS A SUBMISSIVE WOMAN

We have already seen her submission to God when she said, "Yes, Lord, I'm your servant. I'm available." She embraced the will of God though it was completely different from anything she would have planned for her life. Mary also demonstrated her submission to God by her submission to her husband. After Mary's first encounter with the angel, God gave direction for her and for her family through her husband—and she let him lead. To protect his Son from Herod's wrath, God told Joseph to take his family and flee to Egypt. (After what Mary had seen and experienced, it seems she might have found it difficult to take direction from a mere mortal!) After Herod died, God told Joseph to return to Nazareth. As God revealed his will, Joseph led his family, and his family followed.

It's easy for women who are sensitive to the Lord, involved in Bible studies, growing spiritually, and even teaching the Word to others to feel they are more qualified to lead than their husbands and even their pastors. When we communicate this sense of spiritual superiority, we strip men of the motivation to fulfill their God-given calling to provide leadership for their families and for the family of God. If we as women want to fulfill God's purposes for our lives, we must be willing to relinquish control and let God lead through the men he has placed in positions of authority.

MARY WAS AN INFLUENTIAL WOMAN

In the Gospel of John we find the account of Jesus at the wedding feast in Cana. When faced with a shortage of wine, Mary pointed the servants to Jesus: "Do whatever he tells you" (2:5). She used her influence to direct others to Jesus and to encourage them to obey and follow him.

When friends and acquaintances come to us with problems, our role is not to solve their problems but to point them to Jesus and encourage them to "do whatever he tells you."

Mary apparently was also influential in leading her own children to follow Jesus. During his earthly ministry, Jesus' half-brothers did not believe in him (see John 7:5). However, by the time the early church was birthed, they had become believers (Acts 1:14); two of them—Jude and James—penned the New Testament books that bear their names. I believe that Mary was likely one of the key influences in bringing them to faith in Jesus.

MARY WAS A PRAYING WOMAN

She understood the need not only for private prayer but for corporate prayer. After Jesus' ascension into heaven, 120 believers gathered in the upper room for forty days, waiting on God to send the promised Holy Spirit. Mary was among those who "joined together constantly in prayer" (Acts 1:14).

One of the greatest roles in which God has used women as instruments of revival is in the matter of prayer. In 1949–1951 God used two elderly sisters, Peggy and Christine Smith, in the Lewis Revival in Scotland. Both women were in their eighties. Peggy was blind, and Christine was crippled with arthritis. They couldn't even leave their little cottage to worship in the village church. But they knew how to pray. God used their prayers to plant seeds of longing in the hearts of men who then began to pray for revival. God sent a great spiritual awakening in response to the earnest prayers of these two obscure women.

My own life is, to some measure, the fruit of the prayers of a great-grandmother that I never knew. As I read reports of violence and perversion in our culture, as I receive letters from women whose mates and children are far from God, as I look at the backslidden condition of so many of our evangelical churches and homes, I wonder, *Where are the praying women? Where are the wives, mothers, grandmothers, sisters, and daughters who are carrying these burdens on their knees and crying out to God for mercy and divine intervention?*

MARY WAS A DEVOTED WOMAN

She followed Jesus throughout his earthly ministry, even when others rejected or failed to follow him. She was one of the few who followed him all the way to the cross. When others fled for their lives, she remained Jesus' loyal follower, regardless of the personal danger or risk.

As was the case in Jesus' day, many so-called disciples today will follow Jesus as long as it doesn't cost them too much, as long as their family and friends are followers, or as long as they are getting their needs met and following him is rewarding and exhilarating. They are willing to obey the Word when God's ways seem to "work." But few are willing to follow him when it means a cross—when the apparent outcome is not as they had hoped, when they have to live with those who resist him, or when there is no end in sight to the sacrifice and suffering they must endure.

MARY WAS A LOVED WOMAN

Not only did Mary love her Son, but also she was dearly loved by the Lord Jesus. In the final moments of his life, he made sure that his widowed, bereaved mother would be properly and adequately cared for and that her needs would be met. He provided means of grace for her within the context of the family of God. And she accepted his love and his provision for her needs.

As I travel and minister all over the country, I find so many Christian women who feel unloved and emotionally needy. When they look to the things and people of this earth to fill their emotional void, they invariably end up empty and disappointed. No one and nothing can fill that God-sized vacuum. But in the Lord Jesus, we have One who knows and understands us, who loves us fervently, and who cares for us and has provided for our needs. The apostle Paul marveled at the incredible love of Christ:

> Who shall separate us from the love of Christ? Shall tribulation, or distress, or persecution, or famine, or nakedness, or danger, or sword? . . . No, in all these things we are more than conquerors through him who loved us. For I am sure that neither death nor life, nor angels nor rulers, nor things present nor things to come, nor powers, nor height nor depth, nor anything else in all creation, will be able to separate us from the love of God in Christ Jesus our Lord. (Rom. 8:35–39)

The question is, will we believe his promise? Will we let him love us? Will we receive his provision?

MARY WAS A WOUNDED WOMAN

Eight days after Jesus was born, Mary and Joseph took the infant to the temple (Luke 2:21–35). Simeon, who had been waiting for the appearance of the Messiah, took the Christ-Child in his arms and blessed him. Simeon spoke of how the child would be a sign that would be spoken against—foreshadowing the cross and the suffering he would undergo. Then Simeon looked at Mary and spoke words that she would not fully understand until she stood beneath the cross of her son thirty-three years later. On that day she surely remembered Simeon's words, "A sword will pierce through your own soul also" (v. 35).

There at Calvary I believe that sword pierced Mary's soul in more than one sense. First, as a mother she was losing her son. She was giving up his life. Even as he laid down his life, she gave up her son for the salvation and the redemption of the world.

Mothers, have you laid down your children for the sake of Christ and his kingdom? How sad it is on occasion to see Christian parents stand in the way of their children laying down their lives for the sake of Christ. And what a joy to see parents who gladly release their children to the will of God. I remember when a dear pastor's wife, a friend of mine, said good-bye to one of her daughters, along with her son-in-law and two grandchildren, as they left to be missionaries in Cambodia. Just before their departure, I asked my friend, "Isn't this hard for you?" She replied, "Oh, Nancy, I can't think of anything more wonderful than to have a child who wants to lay down her life for the sake of taking the gospel to the world. Yes, it's hard. We won't see them much in this world, but there's a whole lot of eternity after this life." My friend, like Mary of Nazareth, was willing to bear the wounds of giving up her child for God's redemptive purposes.

Another wound pierced Mary's heart—this one even more deeply than the first. You see, she understood that her son was dying not only for the sins of the world, but for *her* sins. Even before he was born, she had recognized him as "God *my* Savior" (Luke 1:47). As good as she was, she was not good enough to get to heaven on her own. As is true with each of us, she had to place her faith in the crucified Son of God who died in her place. As she stood beneath that cross, perhaps she recalled the words of the prophet Isaiah:

> He was wounded for [my] transgressions;
> he was crushed for [my] iniquities . . .
> and with his stripes [I am] healed.
> All we like sheep have gone astray;
> we have turned—every one—to his own way;

and the LORD has laid on him
the iniquity of us all. (Isa. 53:5–6)

Mary was a wounded woman—wounded not only by her suffering, but by her sin. As she gazed upon her crucified son, she realized that he was taking her wounds upon himself. And as she believed, she was healed—cleansed of her sin. Three days later when she learned that he had conquered death and was alive, knowing she had been made whole by his death, she joined the other disciples in taking the good news of his atonement to a wounded, sinful world, that they too might know his healing salvation. For more than 2,000 years Mary's life has provided a portrait of godliness for women who, like her, long to be used of God.

QUESTIONS TO PONDER

As you review the qualities we have seen in the life of Mary of Nazareth, take time to ponder the following questions and ask the Holy Spirit to make you the kind of woman he can use to fulfill his redemptive purposes in your world.

1) *An ordinary woman*: What is it that gives my life significance? Do I believe that God can use my life to make a difference in the world?

2) *A pure woman*: Am I a pure woman? In my behavior? In my relationships? Am I pure in what I watch, read, and listen to? In the way I dress? Am I pure in my motives? My thoughts? My private habits?

3) *An undeserving woman*: Am I conscious that whatever is good or useful about my life is the result of his undeserved grace poured out on me?

4) *A chosen woman*: Am I conscious of having been chosen by God to fulfill a specific purpose in my generation?

5) *A Spirit-filled woman*: Am I depending on the power of the Holy Spirit to be and to do that for which God has chosen me? Am I seeking a fresh, daily filling of his Holy Spirit in my life?

6) *An available woman*: Have I made myself fully available to God for whatever purposes he might want to accomplish in my life? Am I willing for him to use me at any price?

7) *A believing woman*: Am I exercising faith in the promises of God? Am I believing God for that which is impossible apart from his

power? How does my life demonstrate faith in the power of God? What is there about my life that cannot be explained apart from God?

8) *A praising woman*: Is my life characterized by a spirit of praise? Do I respond to the circumstances and challenges of each day by expressing gratitude for the greatness and mercy of God? Do my responses to my daily circumstances give the world a proper view of God?

9) *A woman of the Word*: Do I love the Word of God? Do I read it, memorize it, meditate on it, and share it with others? Do I apply the Word to everyday, real-life situations?

10) *A reflective woman*: Do I take time to remember what God has done and to meditate on what he is doing in my life and in my circumstances?

11) *A humble woman*: Am I content to serve God without human recognition or appreciation? Is it my goal that he might increase and I might decrease? Would I be willing to do all that I do if no one ever saw, applauded, or thanked me?

12) *A trusting woman*: Do I trust God to fulfill his purposes in my life and in the lives of my loved ones? Is there any area of my life where I am trying to work things out on my own rather than trusting God to do what needs to be done?

13) *A submissive woman*: Do I trust God to lead me through the authorities he has placed in my life? Do I make it easy for my authorities to lead me, or am I resistant and stubborn?

14) *An influential woman*: Does my life draw attention away from myself and toward Jesus? How is my life influencing others to love, worship, and obey the Lord Jesus?

15) *A praying woman*: Am I a woman of prayer? Do I consistently join with other believers in praying for the revival of the church and the evangelization of the world?

16) *A devoted woman*: Am I a faithful follower of the Lord Jesus—in the good times and in the bad? Am I committed to following him even when it is costly or when others fail to do so?

17) *A loved woman*: Am I letting Jesus love me, care for me, and meet my needs? Am I receiving the provision he has made to meet my needs?

18) *A wounded woman*: Am I willing to suffer in order that Jesus' redeeming life may be experienced by others? Have I ever trusted in Christ as my Savior, recognizing that the wounds he suffered on the cross were for my sin and for my salvation?

BECOMING A WOMAN
OF DISCRETION

Nancy Leigh DeMoss

IF YOU WERE ASKED TO list the greatest causes for the breakdown of the family, what would you suggest? The culture? The media? Entertainment? Secular education? Anti-family laws and public policy? Urban blight? Poverty? Abusive or absentee fathers?

Would your list include foolish women? The more I study the ways of God, the more sobered I am by the incredible influence we as women have in our homes—for better or worse, for good or evil. The Scripture puts it this way: "The wisest of women builds her house, but folly with her own hands tears it down" (Prov. 14:1). There are two kinds of women in this world—wise and foolish. At any given moment, you and I are either wise or foolish women; whether we realize it, we are either building our "house" or tearing it down.

Every woman has a "house," an immediate sphere of influence. If you are married, if you have children, your family is your closest and most important circle of influence. Single women also have a "house"; it encompasses those lives they touch within their extended family, their church, their workplace, and their community. A wise woman is actively involved in building her house on a daily basis, but the foolish woman tears down her house with her own hands.

John Adams, the second president of the United States, recognized the incredible influence of women, not only on their own homes, but on the entire character of a nation:

The Challenge of Biblical Womanhood

From all that I have read of history and government and human life and manners, I have drawn this conclusion: that the manners of women were the most infallible barometer to ascertain the degree of morality and virtue of a nation. The Jews, the Greeks, the Romans, the Swiss, the Dutch, all lost their public spirit and their republican forms of government when they lost the modesty and domestic virtues of their women.[1]

The destructive influence of foolish women is readily apparent in the secular world. In recent years we have seen the power of foolish women to tear down and destroy the moral sensitivities and fiber of an entire nation. We can all think of high-profile women—entertainers, politicians, wives of public figures—whose philosophies and lifestyles have wielded an enormous, negative influence on our entire culture.

However, what should trouble us even more is the extent to which foolishness among women has permeated the evangelical church. We have followed the world in redefining what it means to be a woman, as well as what it means to be a man. We have blurred, if not eradicated, the distinctions between feminine and masculine character, behavior, and roles. We have lost our moorings, our sense of what is pure and good, true and right. We have little comprehension of the meaning or importance of such old-fashioned words as *wholesome*, *modest*, *discreet*, and *chaste*.

Several years ago I became aware of a situation in which a Christian leader had been involved in inappropriate behavior with a female staff member. When his wife confronted him with her concerns, his response was, "Come on, this is the nineties!" As we have moved into the twenty-first century, there is even greater confusion about such matters. We excuse, tolerate, and justify behavior that would have been unthinkable a generation ago.

At the heart of our current plight is a lack of clear biblical teaching and thinking about our calling and roles as women. Only by returning to the Scripture and placing our lives under its authority can we be delivered from the foolishness that has caused us to tear down our "houses" and become wise women who build our homes. What is at stake is not only our own spiritual well-being, but that of our families, our churches, our communities, and even the generations to come.

Those of us who are "older women" have a responsibility to train the next generation of women in the ways of God: to teach them the characteristics of wise and foolish women, to warn them against the dangers and consequences of being foolish, and to instill in them a vision and commitment to be wise women. We also need to teach our sons and young men the difference between wise and foolish women—what qualities to admire and what qualities to avoid in women.

Proverbs chapter 7 is a technicolor portrait of a foolish woman. The immediate context is that of a father teaching his son how to recognize and be protected from the snare of a foolish woman. However, this passage includes many insights that ought to be an indispensable part of the "curriculum" that we as women master and pass on to the next generation of women.

The first paragraph of the chapter introduces us to the theme. The younger man is urged to embrace wisdom so that he may be protected from a particular kind of woman who has set out to ensnare him.

> *My son, keep my words*
> *and treasure up my commandments with you;*
> *keep my commandments and live;*
> *keep my teaching as the apple of your eye;*
> *bind them on your fingers;*
> *write them on the tablet of your heart.*
> *Say to wisdom, "You are my sister,"*
> *and call insight your intimate friend,*
> *to keep you from the forbidden woman,*
> *from the adulteress with her smooth words. (vv. 1–5)*

The writer warns against becoming entangled with an "adulteress" woman. That word is variously translated "immoral" (NKJV), "adulteress" (NIV), and "strange" (KJV). The word means literally "to turn aside."[2]

The Song of Solomon describes two kinds of women. One is like a "wall"; the other is like a "door" (8:9). The woman who is pictured as a wall has built her life on convictions. As a result, she is firm and unyielding to the wrong kinds of advances from men. She has established her life on the truth of God's Word. The other kind of woman is like a door that can be easily swayed. Because her life is not built on biblical convictions, she is vulnerable to temptation and may well become a temptress herself. The woman in Proverbs 7 is a door. She is loose; she has turned aside from a life of purity and integrity. She is a foolish woman.

Perhaps you are thinking, *I'm not an immoral woman. Proverbs 7 doesn't really apply to me.* I was first encouraged to develop this message for a conference for women who were in full-time Christian ministry. My initial response was, *How could this passage possibly be relevant to those women?*

As I have meditated on this passage, I have come to believe that it is relevant for every Christian woman. First, even in the most respected churches and ministries, there are seductresses—women with adulterous hearts and immoral intent. Any kind of perversion that can be found in the world can also be found in the church today. Just when I think I've heard it all, I become aware of another situation where a Christian home has been shipwrecked on the shoals of immorality. More times than not, there is a loose, foolish woman involved in the tragedy.

Second, in virtually every group of Christian women, there are those who don't realize they are foolish. They are ignorant about the difference between a wise and foolish woman; they do not understand the basics about personal, moral, and relational purity. They need to be trained in the ways of God and discipled to become wise women.

Third, this passage has relevance even for those women who have a genuine heart for wisdom and of whom it could not be said that they are loose or immoral. Sadly, the vast majority of evangelical women have been subtly influenced by the world in ways they don't even realize. The world's way of thinking has infiltrated and permeated the lifestyles of committed church members. Although we may not be physically adulterous or promiscuous, most of us have unwittingly adopted some of the characteristics that ultimately could lead to the ruin and downfall of the men around us. When we look at the characteristics of the foolish woman in Proverbs 7, even if we are not loose, immoral women, we must ask the Lord, "Do any of the characteristics of this woman describe me?"

MARKS OF THE FOOLISH WOMAN

The first characteristic given in verse 5 is that she uses "smooth words." Throughout the Scripture, we see the power of the tongue. Our tongues have the power to destroy our homes and the homes of others. Death and life are in the power of the tongue—the ability to destroy and to heal. The loose woman uses her tongue—her words—to seduce and overpower men. The writer comes back to this theme in verse 21: "With much seductive speech she persuades him; with her smooth talk she compels [KJV, forced] him." You might ask, "How can a tiny, little woman force a man to yield to her?" She does it with her tongue.

> For at the window of my house
>   I have looked out through my lattice,
> and I have seen among the simple,
>   I have perceived among the youths,
>   a young man lacking sense. (vv. 6-7)

The author now begins a blow-by-blow description of exactly how this loose, foolish woman preys on a simple, foolish man who lacks wisdom and understanding. This young man lacks judgment and is careless; he is morally unstable, and the foolish woman is going to take advantage of him. (Of course, the man is also responsible for what transpires in this passage, as in any immoral relationship; but our objective at this point is to focus on our responsibility as women.)

> . . . passing along the street near her corner,
>   taking the road to her house
> in the twilight, in the evening,
>   at the time of night and darkness. (vv. 8-9)

Both the young man and the foolish woman make conscious choices that place them in the wrong place at the wrong time. This passage illustrates the importance of staying away from places and situations where the natural instinct would be to do something wrong. This is a valuable principle for every believer, and one that we ought to teach our young people for their spiritual and moral protection.

Three times the point is repeated that this meeting takes place at night. The pair ends up together alone in the dark. Instead of avoiding the potential of wrongdoing, this foolish man makes his way toward the house where there is a woman with whom he will end up in an immoral relationship. Like magnets they are drawn to each other. They both place themselves in a setting (time and place) where they will be more vulnerable to temptation and sin.

This is why it is so important to guard our steps and our choices in the "little things." The places we go, the books and magazines we read, the music we listen to, the entertainment we watch—these things either fuel our flesh (our natural inclinations) or they nurture our spirit. By the time a full-blown immoral relationship has developed, a woman may have emotions she feels she can't control: "I know I shouldn't be involved with this man, but I can't help the way I feel." Chances are, those feelings were stimulated by foolish choices that she justified to herself and others. The foolish woman places herself in places, situations, and relationships where the potential for wrongdoing exists.

And behold, the woman meets him,
dressed as a prostitute, wily of heart. (v. 10)

Notice that this woman is not actually a prostitute, though she exhibits many of the same characteristics. Verse 14 suggests that she is a "church woman." She is religious; she tries to spiritualize her sensuality and immorality with talk about sacrifices and offerings. She is also a married woman (though either single or married women may fit the description). She is not satisfied with the mate God has provided and has expectations and longings that her husband is not fulfilling (see v. 19). Rather than looking to God to fulfill the deepest needs and longings of her heart, she focuses on what she does not have and looks to others to meet those needs. Rather than pouring love, attention, and devotion upon her husband, she invests her heart, energy, and efforts in another man.

The Proverbs 7 woman is not fictitious. She lives today. She is seen in these kinds of letters that I have received from church women (some details have been changed):

> I have not loved my husband for a long time, and I am miserable. I had an affair three years ago and ended it to stay with my husband for our three young children's sake. Six months ago I began the affair with the same man and have fallen in love with him. I know this is wrong. He's married also, but I can't imagine life without him.

Do you see the foolishness here? This woman is married, but rather than pour her efforts into her relationship with her husband, she has invested her heart elsewhere and consequently has fallen in love with another man. Here's another one:

> I have struggled with Internet addiction. At one point, I was on my computer up to 15 hours a day. It was my way of escaping my empty, lonely marriage. In the last couple of months, I have curbed my Internet usage. I realized I was neglecting our six children and decided to make some changes. However, I met a wonderful man through a chat room. We've met face to face several times now, and I'm considering leaving my husband for this man.

And another:

> My minister and I are very close. Just yesterday, he acknowledged in a counseling session that he was very attracted to me, but he would never act on his desire because he knew that would hurt. Now I feel deeply attracted to him. Help me, Lord, to let go of this, and give me wisdom in setting boundaries. I cut his hair and give him a massage once a month.

Twenty years ago these would have seemed extreme, but not today. I am in churches day after day, week after week, picking up the broken pieces of lives and homes. I often feel like we're dealing with Humpty Dumpty: "All the king's horses and all the king's men cannot put him together again"—save for the grace and power of God. God graciously rescued and restored the woman involved in this last situation, but we need to be teaching women the ways of God on the front end—before they fall into (or cause others to fall into) such traps. Each of these women diverted her attention and affection away from her husband and toward another man, with disastrous consequences.

Verse 10 describes this woman as being dressed "as a prostitute" (the outward manifestation) and as "wily of heart" (the inward attitude that produces the outward manifestation). Our countenance, clothing, choices, and behavior reflect what is in our heart. The heart invariably affects the outward appearance. That is why the foolish woman's dress and her heart are addressed in the same verse.

"Dressed as a prostitute . . . " Though this woman is not a harlot, she is dressed like one. Suggestive, seductive clothing is one of the traps she uses to lure the young man. Immodest clothing is a mark of a foolish woman; modest dress is a mark of a wise, godly woman. Few women today, even in our churches, seem to understand the meaning or importance of modesty. Rather, we have adopted the world's standards and styles. I look around at some gatherings of believers and wonder, *Don't these women realize what they are communicating to men by the way they dress?* Where are the mothers and mature women who are supposed to be modeling and teaching the meaning of modesty? An outwardly modest appearance reflects a modest and wise heart. Immodest dress suggests a foolish, immoral heart.

"Wily of heart"—the foolish woman is subtle of heart. This speaks of being crafty in her intent. She is crafty and has hidden motives. She has set out to ensnare this young man.

> She is loud and wayward;
> > her feet do not stay at home;
> now in the street, now in the market,
> > and at every corner she lies in wait. (vv. 11–12)

The foolish woman has a "loud" or "tumultuous" spirit. Proverbs 9:13 also describes her as "loud" (NKJV, boisterous). She does not exercise restraint or self-control. She is stormy and demanding. Her demeanor is in contrast to the meek and quiet spirit that is priceless to God. Not only is she loud, but she is also "wayward" or "stubborn." She is headstrong and defiant against God's law and against the obligation of morality.

"Her feet do not stay at home." She's a gadabout. In contrast to the wise woman, the foolish woman is not content to be a keeper at home. She is not satisfied with where God has put her. One of the things the feminist movement has done so successfully is to stir up discontent in women with being homemakers and to convince them that other pursuits can increase their sense of self-worth.

My parents married when my mother was nineteen, and my dad was in his early thirties. They had decided not to have children for their first five years of marriage; however, within five years they had six children. My mother adored my father, as he did her, and she loved serving him and our family. She has commented that she didn't know she was supposed to be unhappy until people told her she shouldn't have to deal with all the demands of their busy household.

Fueling discontent and pushing women out of their homes in search of greater meaning and satisfaction has resulted in off-the-chart stress levels for many women who can no longer survive without pills and therapists. The woman whose life does not center on her home and the well-being of her family and who is constantly darting from one place and one activity to another is more vulnerable to becoming entangled in immoral relationships and more likely to entice men who are vulnerable themselves. The greatest spiritual, moral, and emotional protection a woman will ever experience is found when she is content to stay within her God-appointed sphere. This does not mean that she never leaves her house, but rather that her heart is rooted in her home and that she puts her family's needs above all other interests and pursuits.

> **She seizes him and kisses him,**
> **and with bold face she says to him . . . (v. 13)**

This is an all-too-familiar picture in our culture, where women have been trained to be the aggressors in relationships with men. Few women today have any concept of what's wrong with being the initiator. Why shouldn't girls call boys? Why shouldn't they ask young men out for dates? They have never been taught the beauty of God's created order. Even our physiological makeup teaches us that God created the man to be the initiator and the woman to be the responder. Satan's way of doing business is to reverse God's plan. We have a responsibility to teach our young men and women the ways of God in these matters.

The foolish woman in this passage approaches her prey with a bold greeting. She throws herself on this man—physically and verbally. She evidences the lack of discretion and restraint that is so common between men and women today. Even in church it is not unusual to see women casually, carelessly throw their arms around men. Such behavior may not have immoral intent, but it is foolish. At best, it pulls down appropriate restraints that ought to exist between men and women; at worst, it can lead to grave sins against God.

> *"I had to offer sacrifices,*
> *and today I have paid my vows." (v. 14)*

This foolish woman cloaks her aggressive, flirtatious behavior in spiritual talk. Her religious activity is really a cover-up for her immoral heart. She may be trying to compensate for her guilt by what she does at church. Many women in our churches today are active in ministry and Bible study; they leap from one conference to another. Others may think they are spiritual and sincere, but they are covering up foolish hearts and impure behavior.

Proverbs speaks of a man who "was almost in all evil in the midst of the congregation and assembly" (Prov. 5:14, KJV). Even in the midst of church relationships and activities, we can fall into great sin and can lead others into great sin.

> *"So now I have come out to meet you,*
> *to seek you eagerly, and I have found you." (v. 15)*

She builds up this foolish young man's ego; she feeds his need for admiration and makes him feel needed and valued. Whose need for admiration should she be feeding? Her husband's! When she pours admiration on another man, she fuels her discontented feelings about her own husband and intensifies her sense that she is living in an unloving, empty marriage.

> *"I have spread my couch with coverings,*
> *colored linens from Egyptian linen;*

I have perfumed my bed with myrrh,
aloes, and cinnamon." (vv. 16–17)

This woman is consumed with physical, temporal values rather than that which is enduring. She lures this young man into an inappropriate relationship by describing the sensuous nature of her bedroom. Of course, there would be nothing wrong with creating a romantic atmosphere in her bedroom to satisfy her husband. But it is clearly wrong to do so for a man who is not her husband.

The foolish woman is indiscreet—she talks freely about intimate subjects that should be reserved for conversation with her husband. One of the most disconcerting aspects of various highly publicized sex scandals in recent years is the open, candid talk about private matters that has been splashed throughout the news media. Explicit sexual language that was once considered inappropriate outside the bedroom has now become part of our everyday vocabulary. Talk show hosts, entertainers, and journalists seem to pride themselves on exploiting and exposing explicit subject matter. The more intimate the subject matter, the more the audience tunes in. We need to teach young women that there are things you don't talk about in mixed company. Indeed, there are personal matters between husbands and wives that should not be discussed even with other women.

"Come, let us take our fill of love till morning;
let us delight ourselves with love." (v. 18)

The foolish woman does not understand the nature of true love. True love is giving, not getting. Someone has said, "Love can always wait to give, but lust can never wait to get." She is a taker rather than a giver. She seeks immediate gratification, in spite of the fact that the delights of this forbidden fruit will last only "until morning." She fails to think about the long-term consequences of her choices, and as a result she sets up herself and others for moral failure. She is willing to sacrifice her own marriage and integrity, as well as the well-being and future of others, in order to experience a brief taste of the fruit of illicit "love."

Are there ways you have sacrificed long-term gain on the altar of immediate self-gratification? You might not relate to throwing away your marriage for a night of pleasure with another man. But perhaps you can relate to spewing out harsh, angry words that grant some temporary relief but crush the spirit of your mate or your child. Perhaps you know what it is to binge on the food you crave for the momentary pleasure it brings. Perhaps you have indulged your resentful feelings, savoring the thought of hurting the one who hurt you so deeply. Have you seriously considered the long-term consequences of your foolish choices? Have you counted the cost in terms of your relationship with God and with others?

> "For my husband is not at home;
> he has gone on a long journey;
> he took a bag of money with him;
> at full moon he will come home." (vv. 19–20)

Her husband is out of town on a business trip, and she thinks no one will know about her secret little sin. But she forgets that there is One who knows everything—*El Roi*, "the God who sees." She forgets that "The eyes of the LORD are in every place, keeping watch on the evil and the good" (Prov. 15:3).

What "secret little sins" are we indulging in our lives, in our thoughts, in our private moments? How we need to cultivate the fear of the Lord—that constant, conscious sense that we are always under God's watchful eye, whether we are alone or with others.

This woman is apparently seeking to meet "needs" that aren't being met at home. By focusing on her own needs (in actuality, her desires), she puts herself in a position where she is less motivated and capable of meeting the needs of the one whom God created her to help. She was made to be a helper to her husband, but she can't meet his needs if she is focused on her own.

By way of contrast, Proverbs 31 says of the wise, virtuous woman, "The heart of her husband trusts in her, and he will have no lack of gain. She does him good, and not harm, all the days of her life" (vv. 11–12). She has a permanent, unconditional commitment to be loyal to her husband and to act in his best interests.

In today's culture, many women have husbands who are away from home—if not literally and physically, then emotionally, relationally, spiritually, or in terms of their time and focus. The greatest

test of faithfulness for a married woman is where her heart goes when her husband is "away." Where does the woman's mind stray? Where do her thoughts wander? Is she trustworthy? Is she faithful to God and to her calling in marriage even if he fails to be the man he ought to be?

> *With much seductive speech she persuades him;*
> *with her smooth talk she compels him.* (v. 21)

Again, we are reminded of the power of words—flattering, flirtatious, bold, seductive speech. She uses her speech to control. She causes him to yield, just as Delilah used her words to bring Samson under her control. The foolish woman stands in contrast to the wise woman who "opens her mouth with wisdom, and the teaching of kindness is on her tongue" (Prov. 31:26). The wise and virtuous woman uses her tongue to speak words of healing, hope, grace, and help.

THE FRUIT OF THE FOOLISH WOMAN

As we come to the end of Proverbs 7, we see the enormous impact of the foolish woman on others, particularly on men:

> *For many a victim has she laid low,*
> *and all her slain are a mighty throng.* (v. 26)

Feminists have portrayed women as oppressed victims. That is no doubt true in some settings and cultures. However, those situations, no matter how serious, do not relieve us of responsibility for any ways that we may be perpetrators. No failure on the part of men can strip us of accountability for our behavior and for our influence on men, as well as on our entire culture and the next generation.

The foolish woman is an instrument of "[laying] low" *many* men. She may do so by means of sexual seduction, as does the woman in Proverbs 7, or she may do so more subtly, by means of discouragement, spiritual pride, or intimidation. I have found that I can walk into a meeting with a group of men and in a matter of moments change the climate of the room by my spirit. Without even saying a word I can discourage or intimidate the men around me.

Sadly, some of the most "spiritual," biblically knowledgeable women in the church are also the most intimidating. Our generation has been blessed with many Bible study opportunities for women, but if our knowledge makes us unteachable or difficult to live with, we are foolish women. I have heard men say in effect, "I can't lead my wife. I can't lead the women in my church. They know too much." Some of these men feel as though they need advanced theological degrees in order to be the spiritual leaders that their wives claim to want. In many cases I believe that is because our spirits have not been teachable and humble. As a result, we end up emasculating the men around us.

One politically correct way that women lay men low is by verbally bashing them—making "men jokes" or cutting comments about men. Of course, it is equally inappropriate for men to bash women, but the woman is the glory of man (1 Cor. 11:7). When we speak words that cut, diminish, and wound—even in jest—we are tearing down those we were intended to lift up.

"Many a victim has she laid low, and all her slain are a mighty throng." Notice that the men slain by the foolish woman started out as strong men. As a young woman, the Lord used this passage to impress on my heart that if I failed to walk as a wise woman, I could be the instrument of *any* man's undoing, no matter how strong he might be. That was a sobering realization to me. Even men who are spiritually mature can be brought down—controlled, wounded, and destroyed—by a foolish woman.

As I read this passage, I find myself wondering how many wounded or strong men I have cast down—perhaps not morally, but spiritually. How many men have I discouraged or intimidated? Our calling with the men God has placed in our lives is to be a cheerleader, to lift up their hands and to pray for them. Yes, they have weaknesses, as do we; but we need to encourage them and pray and trust God to make them mighty men of God. That is our high and holy calling.

Her house is the way to Sheol,
   going down to the chambers of death. (v. 27)

The consequences of failing to be wise women are deadly. When we are tempted by the immediate pleasures of speaking too freely, letting our emotions and our tongues run wild, or letting our behavior become careless and unrestrained, we need to consider the long-range consequences of our choices.

Some time ago I received an e-mail from a woman who had heard me teach on the foolish woman of Proverbs 7. In this case, the man she had destroyed was her own husband, who had now left her for another woman. By her own admission, her heart had never really been in her home. She had loved her work more than her family and had failed to fulfill her God-given responsibilities as a wife and mother. Now she was living with the lethal consequences of her foolishness.

> I am the epitome of the foolish woman you described. Over and over again, from my earliest childhood, I've been this foolish, adulterous woman. I now see the tragic consequences that have resulted in my husband and in our marriage. I have also planted these vicious seeds in our precious daughter.
>
> I have emasculated my husband, because of my selfish, arrogant, manipulative, intimidating ways and words. How terribly, terribly wounded he is because of me.
>
> I have taken him down to the very core of Hell itself because of my ungodly, willful ways. Today he took the wife of another man to church with him. How could I have driven such a wonderful man to do such a hideous thing before God?
>
> God help me. I see how wrong I've been. I'm trusting in his Word for healing, cleansing, and restoration of my vile heart.

God has brought both this woman and her husband to repentance and is restoring their marriage. What a joy to see this once-foolish woman becoming a wise woman of God. My prayer is that God will make me a wise woman who builds her house for his glory.

> Father, thank you for giving us your Word to teach us how to live as wise women in this godless age. We confess that we have often been foolish women. Please search our hearts and show us any foolish ways that you find, that we may repent and turn to Christ who is our wisdom and our righteousness. Deliver us, O God, from our foolishness. And raise up in our day a new breed of women—holy women; women who trust in you; wise women who will build up their homes. We surrender ourselves afresh to you. May our lives bring you glory and fulfill your purposes here on this earth. In Jesus' name, Amen.

QUESTIONS TO PONDER:
BECOMING WOMEN OF VIRTUE

The following questions (some for married women, some for married and single) have been designed to help us recognize ways that we may be foolish women, and to encourage us to consider practical ways we can become wise women of virtue.

1) Am I building up my "house"—home, workplace, church—or tearing it down?

2) Am I investing in my marriage? Am I nurturing the heart of my marriage?

3) Do I frequently express admiration and gratitude to my husband?

4) Am I reserving the best of my physical and emotional energy for my family?

5) Am I creating a climate (through words, actions, and attitudes) that makes my husband want to be at home?

6) Am I content to be "at home"? Am I finding my fulfillment through reverencing and serving my husband and family?

7) Do I reserve intimate communication, looks, words, and touch for my husband? Am I giving my emotions, attention, or affection to a man other than my husband?

8) Am I meeting my husband's sexual needs?

9) Am I trustworthy? Is there any behavior or relationship I am involved in that I am keeping from my husband? Have I been totally honest with my husband?

10) Does my husband have the freedom to be totally honest with me?

11) Am I taking in sensual thoughts and desires through books, magazines, TV programs, music, or movies that are not morally pure?

12) Have I become a "refuge" for a man who may be struggling in his marriage?

13) Am I looking to a man other than my husband (pastor, counselor, colleague) to be a primary source of counsel or to fill an emotional vacuum in my life?

14) Do I have a more intimate relationship—physically, emotionally, or spiritually—with any man than I do with my husband?

15) Does my demeanor tend to be "loud and defiant," or do I communicate a meek, quiet, and submissive spirit?

16) Am I a "wall" or a "door" (Song 8:9)? Am I a "loose" woman? Do I communicate to the men around me that I am "available"? Does my demeanor invite them to "partake" of intimate parts of

my body, soul, or spirit? Do I engage in flirtatious speech, looks, or behavior?

17) Is there anything about my speech, actions, dress, or attitudes that could defraud the men around me?

18) Am I discreet and restrained in the way I talk with men at work? Is my conversation ever loose, crude, or unbecoming for a woman of God? Am I expressing admiration for a man that should more appropriately come from his wife?

19) Does my dress help men keep their thoughts pure and Christ-centered? Is my dress feminine and modest?

20) Have I erected (and am I maintaining) adequate "hedges" in my relationships with men? What are those hedges?

21) Am I currently in a situation that is (or could become) compromising? Am I in a situation that could appear to others to be compromising?

22) Would my husband, as well as other men and women who know me, say that I am a woman of moral virtue and purity?

23) Have I purposed in my heart to be morally pure? Am I making myself accountable to my husband and to another godly woman for my walk with God and others?

PRUNED TO BLOOM

P. Bunny Wilson

ONCE UPON A TIME there was an old grape branch; it had been growing in the vineyard for a long time. One day a new branch was planted in the next row. The younger branch grew, developed more branches, and bore fruit.

Taking courage one hot summer day, the young branch looked up at the old branch and said in its squeaky voice, "It must be great to have people travel from miles around just to taste the sweetness of your fruit."

The old branch nodded.

Feeling encouraged, the young branch continued, "I have been talking with the other branches in the garden, and they say yours is the sweetest fruit."

The old branch smiled.

"When I grow up, I want to be just like you! How can I have sweet fruit like yours? I'll do anything you say."

As the old branch looked down on the young branch, he remembered the day when, as a young branch himself, he had asked an old branch the same question. In his baritone voice, he gave the young branch the same answer he had received years earlier: "Be willing."

The young branch mused in frustration, *Be willing? I tell him I'll do whatever it takes to have sweet fruit, and all he can say is "Be willing"?* Then he turned to another branch and began carrying on what he felt was meaningful conversation.

Each day there was constant chatter in the vineyard as the branches shared the latest gossip and wasted the hours away by comparing the sweetness of their fruit. The young branch knew there was no other place he'd rather live.

One cool autumn morning, the young branch was awakened by the sound of the old brown, weathered gate opening. As he looked at the end of the row, in stepped the gardener. Normally when the gardener came to visit, the vines would clap their leaves together and shout with delight. But something unusual was taking place that day. A hush swept over the garden. The young branch glanced over at the old branch, who didn't seem to be disturbed; so the young branch directed his attention back to the end of the row.

The gardener stopped by the first branch in the row; the young branch was sure he had come to compliment his friend on her fine growth. But watching intently, he saw the gardener bend on one knee, reach into his back pocket, pull out what looked like sharp scissors, and move toward his friend.

Instinctively the branch at the end of the row pulled her leaves back, and the young branch heard her plead, "No, no, why are you doing this to me? Haven't I been sweet? Didn't I bring honor to the garden? Please, please, don't do this to me!"

Before the young branch could blink, his friend lay on the ground except for the nub. The young branch turned to the old branch and asked in a low, fearful voice, "What's happening? Why did the gardener do that?"

The old branch did not respond.

The young branch strained to understand and then blurted out, "Oh, I get it! We thought the gardener liked that branch, but he really didn't like her."

The old branch responded, "No, that's not true. In fact, what you just saw the gardener do proves he loves that branch."

"Oh. I knew that. Let me try again. We thought that branch's fruit was sweet, but it really wasn't sweet."

"That branch's fruit was sweet."

"Okay, okay; I know the real reason. That branch did something wrong, so the gardener is punishing her; he's just not telling us why."

The old branch answered, "That branch is not being punished. Listen carefully—your friend is being pruned. Not because she was trying to do things wrong, but because she was trying to do things right. Not because her fruit was not sweet, but because the gardener wants it to be even sweeter."

"But that doesn't seem fair!" protested the young branch. "Just look at her. She's been cut down to the nub. Now all the people who come to taste the sweetness of her fruit will laugh and judge the branch."

"Only those outside the garden who don't understand will laugh and judge the branch."

"Only those outside the garden who don't understand? That branch didn't understand! Did you hear her say, 'Why are you doing this to me?'"

The old branch was quiet for a long time and then responded slowly, "Unfortunately, what you're saying is true. It's one thing when people outside the garden don't understand, but when those inside the garden—especially the ones being pruned—don't understand, it causes a lot of confusion, disappointment, and pain. Those branches down at the end of the row will have to listen to your friend murmur and complain until she blooms again."

The young branch proclaimed, "Well, you don't have to worry about being pruned. You have the sweetest fruit in the garden!"

"I want to be pruned."

"You what? It must hurt, and you're going to look funny."

The old branch chuckled and replied, "I must admit it's quite uncomfortable. You see, my young friend, I know I look good to you, but I have a fungus growing on my underside that no one can see. If it remains, it will diminish the quality and quantity of my fruit. No, when the gardener comes to prune me, I won't pull my leaves back. I'll lift myself high in the air to make his job easier."

Trembling, the young branch responded, "I don't understand."

With compassion the old branch replied, "Did you see that branch the gardener just tore off and threw over the fence? It didn't belong in this garden at all and will be burned in a fire."

"Wow!" exclaimed the young branch.

"When the gardener comes to prune you, remember that the gardener only prunes the branches that belong to him, which makes it an honor. He doesn't prune you because you're trying to do things wrong, but because you're trying to do things right. It's not because you're not sweet, but because he wants you to be sweeter. And always remember, my young friend, the very fact that you're being pruned means you will bloom again."

Just then the gardener stopped by the old branch, and the young branch saw the old branch raise his leaves high in the air. He heard a snip, and the old branch lay on the ground except for the nub. Then the gardener turned to the young branch. His leaves were shaking, and tears rolled down his side, but with every ounce of strength he raised his leaves high in the air. He looked up into the gardener's face and said, "Kind and gentle gardener, I'm willing."

FRUIT

Pruning is one of the most important tasks in growing a vineyard. Every year, up to 90 percent of the vine is cut away. A wise gardener knows that pruning positively affects the quantity and quality of the fruit.

The branches are constantly being attacked by diseases, most of which can be kept at bay with pesticides and insecticides. But the vine has to be pruned because there is a deadly fungus that attaches itself to the branch, and its only cure is to be cut out. Each time the vine is pruned, its fruit grows sweeter.

The Scripture often uses an earthly example to explain a spiritual principle. Jesus said, "I am the true vine, and my Father is the vinedresser. Every branch in me that does not bear fruit he takes away, and every branch that does bear fruit he prunes, that it may bear more fruit" (John 15:1–2).

The fruit Jesus is talking about has to do with our Christian disposition, attitude, and temperament. The way we respond when we are pruned reveals our true level of spiritual maturity.

Since you have given your heart to Jesus, are you sweeter? Do you make a sincere attempt to do what is right? Hopefully the answer to these questions is yes. However, even with all your efforts and growth, have you arrived? Are you where he wants you to be? The answer to that question is no. The fact that you have not reached perfection means you will be pruned—regularly. Like that old grape branch, we need to come to the place where we willingly surrender ourselves to be pruned, as uncomfortable as that may be. As the old grape branch would say to the young grape branch, "Remember, you're just being pruned to bloom!"

One of the greatest challenges in the midst of being pruned is dealing with the condemnation that others may heap upon us by suggesting that something is wrong with us unless we are in full bloom all the time. There are always those who are quick to tell us what we are doing wrong and why God is punishing us. Perhaps we don't pray enough, fast enough, or have enough faith. Or maybe God is exacting revenge for one of our shortcomings. So on top of being cut down to a nub, we must sometimes endure the misunderstanding of well-meaning friends. That part of the pruning process can be the most painful.

SEASONS FOR PRUNING AND BLOOMING

We usually find ourselves in one of three places: we have just been pruned, we are growing back after a pruning, or we are in full bloom. Perhaps everything is going right in your life. Enjoy yourself, but remember that the fact you are not perfect means you will be pruned again. That knowledge will keep you humble during blooming season.

Or maybe you are growing after a pruning. Your growth will be stunted if you spend your time looking back on your last pruning with regret instead of gratitude. It can be tempting to walk in unforgiveness and bitterness over an unpleasant occurrence that was part of your pruning. Let me encourage you to let it go as you rejoice in the strength gained to move on to the next level.

Or perhaps you have recently been pruned—cut down to the nub. You look funny, and it hurts. Be patient, and the pain will pass. Rejoice that the fungus has been cut away and in time you will bloom again. Don't stunt your growth with "What if . . . ?" or "If I had only . . . " Stop asking God, "Why?" and start thanking him and rejoicing in his infinite wisdom, for he knows what is best for you. You will then discover your discomfort quickly dissipating.

THAT INCURABLE FUNGUS

That of which we need to be pruned never goes away in this world. It will be with us until we die. No matter how much we love the Lord, it will always be present. It is incurable and often undetected with the human eye. Like a fungus on a vine, it attaches itself to our spiritual underside and often appears in the most unexpected places. That insidious intruder is self—our flesh, which demands to have its way.

> For the desires of the flesh are against the Spirit, and the desires of the Spirit are against the flesh, for these are opposed to each other, to keep you from doing the things you want to do. (Gal. 5:17)

The flesh (self) will not go away in this life, and it will always cause us to suffer because it takes us away from God's plan for our lives. When we surrender to the desires and demands of our flesh, our hearts are turned away from the Lord and toward self-satisfaction. But how can we readily recognize self so we can respond to it quickly and avoid unnecessary pain and pruning? The apostle Paul admonishes us, "But if we judged ourselves truly, we would not be judged" (1 Cor. 11:31).

Self can usually be identified by what we are trying to control and what is controlling us. In one instance we are playing God, and in the other we are refusing to believe there is a God who will help us.

Just what are you trying to control? If you are single, are you attempting to determine when and how you will meet "Mr. Right"? Are you frustrated and despondent? Then you are trying to maintain control. It is important to remember that for every *godly* single woman who *desires* a godly spouse, there is one. The emphasis is on the words *godly* and *desire*. If you are godly, you want to please God; you don't want to break his heart. You would deny yourself rather than knowingly go against his will as revealed in his Word. And true desire allows God to place his desire for your life in your heart. If his desire is for you to be married, he will answer his own desire. *He* will make it happen in his time and in his way. Frustration is thus replaced with patient anticipation, knowing that he is in control.

Maybe you are a single parent and are trying to control (manipulate) your children. If so, you are probably at the end of your rope. God didn't design you to be both a father and a mother for your children. He created you to be the nurturer, though that doesn't mean you ignore the need for biblical discipline. You must establish clear guidelines, be consistent in your response to both negative and positive behavior, and devote as much time as possible to nurturing your children. When they get out of hand, let them know you are going to talk to their Father. You don't have to scream and yell; simply excuse yourself to the privacy of your bedroom, and they will know you are talking to God about them. Let him deal with your children. Teach them that the Lord is your source and your strength. You will be surprised at how God works in their hearts and at the peace that will fill your home.

You may be separated from your husband and find yourself in a terrible state of mind—torn between two forces, one suggesting you end it all and the other trying to hold on to the possibility that it may work out. Let me encourage you to release the situation into the Lord's hand. Your husband not only needs his mind changed—his heart needs to be changed, and only God can do that. Take one day at a time, and cultivate a grateful spirit for God's blessings. Wait on God to work out your situation in his way and in his time. When you relax and give your marriage to the Lord, you will respond differently when you are around your husband. Your conversation and your actions and reactions will be under his control. Don't get ahead of God or try to tell him what to do. Live in quiet assurance that he has the situation under control.

You may be a widow and have to go on without your spouse. Now is the time to release all your gifts and talents into the hands of the Lord so that he can direct your path. You will discover that this can be one of the most productive times in your life. Don't try to control loved ones and others around you in order to get them to fill your void. Move on and discover all God has for you during this season.

You may be married and have discovered that your husband refuses to be controlled. If he would just listen to your "constructive criticism" and change, everything would be perfect in your marriage!

I tried for years to fix my husband but found him to be an unwilling participant. My controlling spirit was a fungus that needed to be cut away, and I received many prunings for it. When I stopped trying to control him and instead determined to focus on his strong points, he began to positively develop in the areas of my concern. I learned the truth of the biblical promise that "he who began a good work in you [in my husband and in me!] will bring it to completion" (Phil. 1:6).

IT'S GROWING

The self fungus will never leave us alone while we are here on earth. It will constantly try to attach itself to us, and we must be determined to fight it. Many times it is fueled by our archenemy, the Devil. For this reason the Scripture says, "Be sober-minded; be watchful. Your adversary the devil prowls around like a roaring lion, seeking someone to devour" (1 Pet. 5:8).

When God prunes us, the result will be greater growth and sweeter fruit. When the Devil attacks us, his intention is destruction. It is important to know the difference. As believers we must understand that Satan can ask God's permission to prune us in some way, but the Devil has the power to do so only if God allows it. Isn't it wonderful to know Satan cannot do just anything he desires to us? I'm sure we would all be sick or dead if he had his way. Do you remember the story of Job? It is a perfect picture of God's sovereign control over Satan in the pruning process:

> Now there was a day when the sons of God came to present themselves before the LORD, and Satan also came among them. The LORD said to Satan, "From where have you come?" Satan answered the LORD and said, "From going to and fro on the earth, and from walking up and down on it." And the LORD said to Satan, "Have you considered my servant Job, that there is none like him on the earth, a blameless and upright man, who fears God and turns away from evil?" Then Satan answered the LORD and said, "Does Job fear God for no reason? Have you not put a hedge around him and his house and all that he has, on every side? You have blessed the work of his hands, and his possessions have increased in the land. But stretch out your hand and touch all that he has, and he will curse you to your face." And the LORD said to Satan, "Behold, all that he has is in your hand. Only against him do not stretch out your hand." So Satan went out from the presence of the LORD. (Job 1:6–12)

The Lord allowed Satan to do unpleasant things to one of his most faithful followers. And Job's endurance led to his enlightenment and finally his restoration. Truly he was pruned to bloom.

Pruning usually takes place when God uses situations, people, and circumstances to help mature us in our Christian disposition, attitude, and temperament. In 1998 I developed a tremor in my right hand. After many tests and consultations, the specialists were still baffled by my situation. What was I to do? I had confirmed speaking engagements and radio and television interviews. Should I cancel? Was this God's way of telling me that he no longer wanted me in the public eye? The temptation was to pull back my leaves, ask God "Why me?" and beg him not to allow this to happen.

I was not afforded the luxury of the apostle Paul who knew why he was afflicted: "*To keep me from becoming conceited* because of the surpassing greatness of the revelations, a thorn was given me in the flesh, a messenger of Satan to harass me, to keep me from becoming conceited" (2 Cor. 12:7). I did, however, learn from Paul's example when he explained how he handled his pruning. He continues:

> Three times I pleaded with the Lord about this, that it should leave me. But he said to me, "My grace is sufficient for you, for my power is made perfect in weakness." Therefore I will boast all the more gladly of my weaknesses, so that the power of Christ may rest upon me. For the sake of Christ, then, I am content with weaknesses, insults, hardships, persecutions, and calamities. For when I am weak, then I am strong. (vv. 8–10)

There we have it. As this book goes to print, I have not missed one speaking engagement or one radio or television interview. It has taken quite an adjustment. I can no longer hold a microphone and walk back and forth. I have to stay fixed behind a podium with a small object turning in my hand the whole time so that my tremor can be somewhat controlled. The result? People love Handy and me.

Who is Handy? That is my tremor. I show audiences my trembling hand and say, "You may have noticed that my hand is shaking. It's a tremor, and I call it 'Handy' because it comes in handy for seasoning food, scratching backs, and tickling my daughter. It is also handy for reminding me to pray without ceasing, to seek God's face, and to go to the secret places with God."

When one lady suggested that the Devil made my hand tremor, I responded, "The only way Satan can touch me is to get permission from God. Maybe he did ask for the right to make my hand shake; but if he did, he's been begging God ever since to make it stop, because not only does it remind me to pray, but when others see the tremor, it reminds them to pray. So that makes me a walking prayer machine!"

Handy has also been a blessing in teaching my children how to face life's unexpected challenges. My nine-year-old, Gabrielle, loves Handy. What if I had pulled back from this pruning and been ashamed? How might she have reacted? Would she have hesitated to introduce me to her friends? I'm sure it would have added strain and pressure to her life. But now when I visit her school, she introduces Handy to her friends. She doesn't realize it now, but as she grows older, the example of how to positively handle affliction will be at her disposal.

Perhaps you have a Handy that can't be seen with the human eye. Something in your life is shaking. Maybe it's an internal illness, or perhaps it is a mental, emotional, financial, or even relational circumstance. God wants you to take a look at your Christian attitude, temperament, and disposition. Is it pleasing to him? If not, let me encourage you to stop reading, ask God to forgive you, and receive his grace. Then take your Handy and let it draw your focus to the living Savior. Allow it to be an ongoing reminder that he is in control and that "all things work together for good, for those who are called according to his purpose" (Rom. 8:28).

RAISING OUR BRANCHES

Where are you being pruned in your life today? Are you filled with confusion, fear, and murmuring? Have you been asking, "Why me?" Why not raise your branch high in the air, look into the face of your wise, heavenly Father, and say, "Kind and gentle gardener, I'm willing"?

PART THREE

The Freedom and Joy of Women as Helpers and Nurturers of Life

A WIFE'S RESPONSIBILITY TO HELP HER HUSBAND

Barbara Hughes

Reprinted and updated from the book Disciplines of a Godly Woman *(Crossway, 2001)*

The LORD God said, "It is not good that the man should be alone; I will make him a helper fit for him."
GENESIS 2:18

EVERY GENERATION HAS BROUGHT its expectations to marriage. My own mother, when she married in 1934, planned a beautiful wedding and looked forward to a life of helping and respecting her husband, who would love her and provide for their family. What actually happened during the forty-six years of my parents' marriage did not live up to either one's expectations, and yet each of them would have counted their marriage a success—and a blessing.

A SUCCESSFUL MARRIAGE?

On a sunny April morning in 1934, a California family gathered flowers and greenery in their well-tended garden in preparation for the wedding of their much-loved daughter, Lula Anne. The bride, her mother and father, five younger sisters and a brother, aunts, uncles, and cousins helped hang garlands and fashion an arbor of roses under which the shy couple would stand before the minister and make their holy vows the next day.

That night, exhausted after long hours of hard work and laughter, they fell into bed in eager anticipation. To their disappointment, they awoke to the dark, thunderous downpour of a spring storm. The garlands had been ripped from the branches and the arbor toppled by the high winds. Plans hastily changed. They prepared the house for the festivities in what little time remained before the ceremony would begin. The few photos of that event were snapped when the rain stopped momentarily and everyone dashed outside. They show a young man and woman in black and white against a background of gray, an image of a marriage beginning.

The best man and his wife planned to drive the couple to their honeymoon destination—no simple task in 1934. The California coast highway to Santa Barbara was roughly paved, and the car's inferior tires resulted in more than one unplanned stop. After several hours the wedding party was too weary to complete the drive. They parked at the side of the road and fell asleep. In the dark of that first night the bride's suitcase was quietly lifted out of the car as they slept. The thief took the few precious things she'd saved up for her wedding night. For the second time in less than twenty-four hours, the young bride, my mother, cried.

Father's name was Wilfred. He had a twin brother named Willard, and everyone on the farm called them "Will-Work" and "Won't-Work." From childhood my father worked hard and valued a job well done. As a child, I remembered that nickname as I observed the amazing energy he brought to any task. An unskilled laborer, he worked at whatever job was available—as a gardener at a bird sanctuary, digging ditches for highway drainage systems, and most often in the lumberyards. The nature of the work often put him in danger, and he suffered more than one serious accident.

After the birth of my younger sister, a load of lumber fell on Dad and crushed his ankle. Even with a huge cast on his leg, he was determined to work, hobbling around to help Mom hang out the laundry. During that time, my mother drove an ice cream truck from nine in the morning until nine at night to provide our family of seven with six dollars a day—enough to feed us, barely. My mother and father simply did what was necessary. I'm sure there were tears, but I rarely saw them.

When I was twelve, my father became a Christian. Among my most treasured memories is the day of his conversion when he came through the door with a tearstained face and hugged my mother. Those were the happiest days of my childhood. Dad would report regularly at dinner how he was working to clean up his language and how his coworkers teased him. He'd recall his attempts to witness to his buddies. Most of all, he radiated joy.

That summer the church I'd been attending on my own had its annual all-church picnic, and for the first time Mom and Dad came. There was fried chicken and potato salad, apple pie, and watermelon. Dad played volleyball with his Sunday school class. His laughter still echoes in my soul.

The day after the picnic there was another accident at the lumberyard. This time my dad nearly lost his hand to a power saw. The following year he endured many surgeries. While undergoing physical therapy, he memorized Scripture. He received a leather New Testament with his name inscribed in gold as first prize in his Sunday school class memory contest.

As difficult as the physical pain had been to endure, the pain that faced my father in the days ahead was far greater. Now this hard-working laborer could no longer use his hands to provide for his wife and children. The attorneys protected the interests of the lumber company, and my father was left crippled and penniless. From the day the court handed down the decision, my father worked at the only job he could get—washing dishes.

My older sister recalls a day in a restaurant when she was out with friends, and a pitcher of Coke was knocked over. Laughing and having a grand time, they barely noticed the arrival of the man sent to clean up the mess. As he mopped, my sister looked up into the anguished eyes of our father. She was humiliated, and he was tortured by her embarrassment.

With his role as provider stripped away, my father grew increasingly depressed. He began drinking heavily. Eventually he ended up on skid row in Los Angeles. During the years that he was separated from our family, people told my mother to give up on Dad. She didn't;

she clung to her chosen role of helping and respecting her husband by ensuring that we children spoke of our father with love and respect. When he was diagnosed with emphysema, he came home. Mother lovingly nursed him the last eleven years of his life.

My children's memories of their grandfather are from those eleven years. They adored him—this cheery invalid who made great chili and loved Grandma. My father died blessing my mother, as well as the Lord she had so faithfully followed in obedience to the vows she had taken those many years before.

When Dad died, my mother wept. The lover with whom she had shared so much—love, pain, sacrifice, failure, disappointment, forgiveness, laughter, and hope—the partner with whom she'd shared the sweetness and challenges of parenthood was gone.

But there were also tears of joy because my mother had the satisfying knowledge that they had ended well. In spite of the many difficulties of their journey together, Mom and Dad parted without bitterness, leaving their children a heritage of blessing.

By today's standards, and indeed compared to the humble hopes they'd begun with, my parents lacked all the things deemed necessary for success in marriage. Father had received no earthly reward for his hard work, much less for his good intentions and desire to be a Christian husband after he was converted. Disaster was followed by despair—for long, lost years. Mother, who had never anticipated being a single parent or the family's sole breadwinner, found herself in that lonely situation.

But my mother's faithfulness to her marriage vows, made before God, preserved her marriage. Her faith in Christ helped her to serve, respect, bless, and forgive her husband.

A BIBLICAL STANDARD FOR A WIFE'S ROLE

Surprisingly, in a time when Christians have more money and more education and certainly more resources such as books, videos, counselors, and support groups to advise them, many young couples lack the most important ingredient for the success of their Christian union—a biblical understanding of their roles. Certainly the time-honored passages of Scripture that teach married people how to relate to one another haven't changed. But the church's shifting view of that teaching has left couples indecisive and confused.

Consider, for example, the way marriage vows have changed over the years. Sentimental and generic, they typically lack a solidarity with the past that reflects the lifelong commitments made by our parents and grandparents. Historically, the Christian marriage vows were rooted in Scripture, especially in the last half of Ephesians 5. Every Christian couple ought to understand and, I think, even commit to memory the directives given there. Those sacred words compass the foundational discipline of marriage, teaching us that the marital relationship must reflect that of Christ and his bride, the church. Christ and his holy church model the sacrificial love and submission that we seek to build into our marriages.[1]

Hear God's Word: "Wives, submit to your own husbands, as to the Lord. For the husband is the head of the wife even as Christ is the head of the church, his body, and is himself its Savior. Now as the church submits to Christ, so also wives should submit in everything to their husbands. . . . And let the wife see that she respects her husband" (Eph. 5:22–24, 33b).

The apostle Paul calls this a "profound mystery." The mystery is more than profound. It is spectacular! The mystery of marriage did not begin when Christ came and established His church. It began centuries before. It was God's plan from the beginning. So if you want to understand the New Testament teaching on marriage, you must begin with the Genesis account of creation.

THE OLD TESTAMENT FOUNDATION

In her best-selling book *A Return to Modesty*, young Jewish author Wendy Shalit argues that "people today have missed the fact that our differences are key to our relationship." She explains: "The sexual revolution seems to have failed mostly because it ignored the differences between the sexes. . . . Not only do we think there are differences between the sexes, but we think these differences can have a beautiful meaning—a meaning that isn't some irrelevant fact about us but one that can inform and guide our lives. That's why we are swooning over nineteenth-century dramas and clothing."[2]

She's right. And we who believe God's Word don't have to guess or wonder about the meaning of those differences. The first chapters of the book of Genesis give us a "better understanding of the profound and complex order which makes sense of the differences between men and women,"[3] and therefore of the roles of husband and wife.

UNITY

The intriguing words of Genesis 1:26 provide essential information about God—and because we are made in his image, about ourselves. Listen to the mystery in God's declaration: "Let us make man in our image." When God speaks of himself in the plural ("us"and "our"), we learn that though God is One, he is not alone. Whatever else it may mean to be made in God's image, this verse makes it clear that we are made for relationship.

The astonishing truth then is: "Like God, mankind is both unified and diverse. We know from the rest of Scripture that the three persons of the Godhead (Father, Son, and Holy Spirit) are nevertheless a single God, and that from all eternity they have enjoyed relationship with each other. Mankind is created in this image, with separate persons (male and female) created to enjoy a deep unity."[4]

This unity goes deeper than the bond with one's own flesh and blood. The moment I held each of my newborn children in my arms, a powerful bonding took place. They were from my flesh. I am close to them, interwoven with them. Yet I am not "one flesh" with them; I am one flesh only with my husband. The sexual union between husband and wife makes two literally become one—body and soul. As the years go by, we become more and more one flesh as there is an exchange of soul, a mutual appropriation of each other's lives.

Genesis 1:27 goes on to say: "So God created man in his own image, in the image of God he created him; male and female he created them." The use of the biological terms "male" and "female," rather than "man" and "woman," shine a spotlight on gender differences—physiology and function. Understanding the differences will help us appreciate Paul's command in Ephesians to "submit to" and "respect" our husbands. Such an understanding will give young women what Wendy Shalit is looking for—a sense of the relevance of gender differences to their lives.

DIVERSITY

In the words of Claire Smith in her article "Two Commands to Women," "God is a God of order, and we were created for relationships that reflect his order and purpose."[5] Even within the Trinity there is an order to the relationship. Scripture reveals differences in the roles of the Father, the Son, and the Holy Spirit. These differences are not demeaning. Theologian Wayne Grudem explains it like this: "It is the Father that planned redemption and sent his Son into the world; the Son obeyed the Father, accomplishing redemption for us; and the Spirit brings to completion the work that has been planned by the Father and begun by the Son. The Father directs and has authority over the Son, and the Son obeys and is responsive to the directions of the Father. The Holy Spirit is obedient to the directives of both the Father and the Son."[6]

Made in God's image, men and women are also equal but different. Equal before God as persons, we have been given distinctly different roles. In the marriage relationship, man is to lead, and woman is to follow his lead. In the beginning Eve rebelled against God, rejecting his will regarding the forbidden tree, and then encouraged her husband to follow her lead. When Adam joined her, failing to lead his wife in godliness, they overturned the good order of creation. Ever since that day there has been war between the sexes.

COUNTERCULTURAL WOMEN

To live out biblical standards for roles in marriage, however, is to swim upstream against culture. And it's not only secular society that angrily reacts against the idea of differing roles. There is also widespread confusion among believers on Scripture's teaching on the subject. A recent article in the *Chicago Tribune* quoted a woman from a Christian organization: "[We do] not believe that marriage is about subordination, but mutuality. Intimacy is impossible when you subordinate to anybody else. That is not what the Bible says, and we don't think that's how God intended us to live."[7]

Excuse me! We know from the very first book of the Bible that "intimacy through subordination" is not only possible, but it is God's plan for us—modeled after the intimacy that exists in the Godhead.

So for me, as a Christian woman, submitting to my husband is not an option; it is obediently following God's plan for order in marriage, a plan that has existed from the beginning.

The wonder of my wedding night—my face warm with the flush of timidity and embarrassment that came with the vulnerability I was experiencing for the first time—is a sweet, lingering memory. My husband and I had begun to explore the mystery that God wondrously provided for us. From the beginning God made us in his image, male and female—equal but different. And when we women live out this profound mystery, we are pleasing God by living out his beautiful order.

There's only one problem, and it's a big one: we don't live in an ideal world or with ideal men who perfectly follow the Ephesian instruction to love their wives as Christ loved the church and laid down his life for her. Like Adam, many husbands fail to lead (or sacrificially love). And like Eve, many wives rationalize about submission, inwardly mouthing Satan's condescending question, "Surely God didn't really say that!"

But God did say it, and the New Testament's passages on marriage consistently root their teaching in Genesis.

NEW TESTAMENT GUIDANCE

Three of the New Testament passages that call women to submit to their husbands include an important and instructive phrase. Ephesians 5:22 says, "Wives, submit to your husbands as to the Lord." Colossians 3:18 similarly reads, "Wives, submit to your husbands, as is fitting in the Lord." These parallel phrases serve as reminders to all wives that submission in marriage must be with the same loving wholeheartedness with which we submit to the Lord. When we submit to our spouses, we are once again agreeing with God that his beautiful ordered plan is worth obeying and the mystery worth preserving. By so doing we once again acknowledge that Jesus is Lord.

The third passage, 1 Peter 3:1, says, "Likewise, wives, be subject to your own husbands . . . " This essential term from Peter, "likewise," holds the key to empowering us to do what we ought when it seems impossible.

In the chapter that precedes 1 Peter 3 (1 Peter 2:13–25), Peter teaches all believers that submission to every authority instituted by God is essential. "For this is the will of God, that by doing good you should put to silence the ignorance of foolish people," states 1 Peter 2:15. The apostle goes on, "If when you do good and suffer for it you endure, this is a gracious thing in the sight of God" (v. 20). God's will and pleasure are always the defining factors for behavior choices.

Wonderfully, Peter points to Christ as an example of the beauty and effectiveness of submission:

> For to this you have been called, because Christ also suffered for you, leaving you an example, so that you might follow in his steps. He committed no sin, neither was deceit found in his mouth. When he was reviled, he did not revile in return; when he suffered, he did not threaten, but continued entrusting himself to him who judges justly. He himself bore our sins in his body on the tree, that we might die to sin and live to righteousness. By his wounds you have been healed. For you were straying like sheep, but have now returned to the Shepherd and Overseer of your souls. Likewise, wives, be subject to your own husbands . . . (1 Pet. 2:21–3:1)

It could be that you and I have often read this command to wives as a stand-alone idea, apart from the preceding verse. But "in the same way" connects us to the example and person of Jesus! We are to submit to our husbands in the same way that Christ submitted to God's will and went to the cross; He "continued entrusting himself to him who judges justly." Jesus' persistent faith in God's goodness and wisdom in everything was unflinching. Obedience to God's will was his primary concern.

Obedience to God's will was Eve's point of failure. She doubted God's goodness and wisdom in denying her the tree of the knowledge of good and evil. Through the gospel, we who are Eve's daughters are now also children of God, and we've been given the power to live like Christ. But obedience is still up to us.

Submission to our husbands begins and ends with trusting God. My mother began and ended by trusting God—no matter how dark her trials. I cannot recall her ever questioning God's love or care for her or for her family.

So that word that today's Christian women struggle over, *submit*, is still God's Word for us: "Likewise, wives, be subject to your own husbands."

HELPER

From the very beginning, a woman's purpose was clearly defined. God took a look at Adam and said, "Then the LORD God said, 'It is not good that the man should be alone; I will make him a helper fit for him'" (Gen. 2:18). So why does our blood pressure rise at the mention of the word *helper*? It's a cultural norm for us to associate weakness and even inferiority with the one who assists. No one wants to play second fiddle. But the fact is, without a second violin there is no harmony.

What is helping supposed to look like—then and now? With what task, for instance, was Eve supposed to help Adam? She was to assist him in carrying out God's order to rule and subdue the earth. But she failed God when she led Adam to join her in submitting to Satan. We modern daughters of Eve must not fail as did our mother. Our task is to encourage our husbands to obey God's Word and will for their lives.

I first began to understand this concept in a personal way when my husband was a young pastor in California. I'd noticed that when things were going well at church, he was pretty upbeat; but when things went wrong, he was easily discouraged. If church attendance was up, he was up; if it was down, so was he. Then the numbers went down—for a long time. He didn't confide in me, but he was seriously wondering whether he should continue in the pastoral ministry.

One night after the children were soundly sleeping, he began to reveal his misery to me. My attempts to console him were met with depressing responses. When I said, "Honey, your sermon really spoke to me last week," he responded, "Yes, but I'll just be on trial again next week." I tried again: "Just think of Noah. He preached 120 years without a single convert!" Kent's dark-humored response was, "Yes, but there wasn't another Noah across town with the people flowing into his ark."

Finally I stopped offering advice and simply listened. The words he spoke that night were those of a man who had lost sight of what biblical ministry is all about. A combination of secular ideas presented to us by church growth experts coupled with his own fear of failure had propelled Kent into a desperate search for success. As he recited his negative observations of ministers and ministry in general, he found himself coming to a conclusion he didn't want to admit. It had been growing in him for a long time, and it was terrible: "God has called me to do something he hasn't given me the gifts to accomplish. Therefore, God is not good." In aching desperation he asked me, "Barbara, what am I going to do?"

When we think back to that long-ago night, Kent tells me that if I had answered him in any other way than the way I did, it would have been all he needed to "hang it up." If I had joined him in bitter recriminations and complaints about our situation, he might have quit the ministry and spent the rest of his life attempting to prove his worth and God's injustice.

But, thanks to God, my answer was full of hope in God. "I don't know what you're going to do, but for right now, for tonight, hang on to my faith, because I believe. I believe that God is good. I believe that he loves us and is going to work through this experience. So hang on to my faith. I have enough for both of us."

Together we turned to the Bible, searching for God's view of success. Together we found it—and it didn't look much like the up-and-down numbers game we'd been playing. The truths we found have served as a polestar in our life that we return to together again and again. Whether it be marriage or ministry, success is defined by knowing and obeying God's will as revealed in his Word.

This was the first time that I became aware of the powerful role I have as my husband's helper. It was also at this time that I discovered something beautiful about gender roles. In John 14:16 Jesus comforts his disciples with the promise of the Holy Spirit, referring to him as "another Helper." By addressing the Holy Spirit as a helper, Jesus forever elevated the position of the one who assists. Trace the Holy Spirit's actions through the New Testament, and you'll find the Spirit repeatedly encouraging, comforting, coming alongside, and helping. The work of the Holy Spirit, the Helper, is beautiful! And women are never more regal and lovely than when they follow his example, cherishing their responsibility as helpers.

So Christian wives must never resent or despise the term *helper* or consider it demeaning. To help is divine! There is no better word to describe the role of a wife than *helper*.

A GENTLE AND QUIET SPIRIT

Most women today care something about the way they look; beauty is so important to our society! But again God's idea of what's beautiful is countercultural. The beauty God desires for wives is the result of trust and obedience—a gentle and quiet spirit.

> Do not let your adorning be external—the braiding of hair and the putting on of gold jewelry, or the clothing you wear—but let your adorning be the hidden person of the heart with the imperishable beauty of a gentle and quiet spirit, which in God's sight is very precious. For this is how the holy women who hoped in God used to adorn themselves, by submitting to their own husbands, as Sarah obeyed Abraham, calling him lord. And you are her children, if you do good and do not fear anything that is frightening. (1 Pet. 3:3–6)

Gentleness, or meekness as many translations have it, isn't weakness or spinelessness or timidity or even niceness. This word in classical Greek was used to describe tame animals, soothing medicine, a mild word, and a mild breeze.[8] It is a word with a caress in it.[9]

Gentleness also implies self-control. Aristotle said that gentleness is the mean between excessive anger and excessive angerlessness. So the person who is gentle is able to balance his anger. He controls it.

Meekness/gentleness is strength under control.[10] The gentle woman is strong! She is in control of her fears. She is as strong as steel. Jesus tells us in the third Beatitude, "Blessed are the meek, for they shall inherit the earth" (Matt. 5:5). Jesus calls himself gentle: "Take my yoke upon you, and learn from me, for I am gentle and lowly in heart, and you will find rest for your souls" (Matt. 11:29). And in 1 Peter the holy women of old, and in particular Sarah, are examples of this gentle beauty. We learn from 1 Peter 3, then, that Sarah's gentle and quiet spirit was a direct result of her trust in God while submitting to her husband.

This is a beauty that most of us living in the early part of the new millennium hear little about. We have plenty of magazines and exercise gear infomercials to keep us up-to-date on how to cultivate beauty and keep our bodies fit and trim. We take skin care very seriously—using exotic ointments and lotions to protect us from exposure that causes premature wrinkles. We make sure we are color-coordinated. And if our bank account permits, we seek procedures that offer a few more years of youthful appearance. We do all of this in the pursuit of the beauty the world esteems and yet ignore the convicting passages of Scripture that tell us where the beauty that God values resides.

RESPECT

Earlier we touched on that important passage on marriage in Ephesians 5. The end of that passage focuses attention on another wifely attribute that God considers important: ". . . and let the wife see that she respects her husband" (Eph. 5:33b).

Most women seem to think their husbands must earn respect before wives can give it. They couldn't be more wrong. Even when a husband is utterly not respectable, his wife can honor him by respecting his position. Sarah understood this: "She lived with a flawed man who asked her to do something unthinkable, yet she didn't hold this horrendous failure over him the rest of his life but restored her respect for him in her heart and lived with him, calling him, 'Master.'"[11]

Remember the story of my mother? Just as she never questioned God's goodness and care for us, she seemed always to hold fast to her love and respect for Dad. She wouldn't tolerate bad talk about him from us children or from anyone else. I have no memory of her ever speaking a critical word about my father. Even when he was at his worst—which could be pretty bad—he could always be sure that Mom's love and respect for him was steady.

My mother's spirit paid off in a surprising dividend over time to the marriage and the family. Because of her faithfulness and forgiveness he was restored to our family for those eleven years before he died. Because of Mother's choice to respect Dad, her children and grandchildren have memories of a positive relationship with him. We remember the little things—like huge anniversary cards with the almost illegible script of his crippled hand, and dinners prepared with great effort for her to come home to after her work as a janitor at a preschool.

Too often these days we hear of love that is only conditional: "I'll love you as long as you love me." But my mom understood that real love stands apart from circumstances and sees the object of love with all its flaws—and loves anyway. Real love is intentional, an act of the will. It's respect that's given because it's the Lord who requires that respect be given.

When I hear women whining about their husbands' faults to friends, and I catch myself speaking to my husband in tones that don't sound honoring, I want to shout, "Stop! Stop yourself, Barbara! Think of the consequences!" Our attitudes and words are teaching the next generation.

Where have you learned to speak to and about your husband? From television talk shows or sitcoms—or from God's Word? Giving loving respect to your husband—even when he doesn't deserve it—is God's will. Watch your actions and listen to your words. God sees and hears.

A GOAL FOR LIFE AS A WIFE

When Eve was tempted, she wanted what God in his goodness had not given her. Things haven't changed. Sometimes I desire an easier, quieter life. At times I long to be free from other people's problems. And I despair at the constant bombardment of voices telling me I should pursue personal power and prestige. I know such thinking is foolish. A wise woman once told me that today's woman in search of equality often overlooks the one thing she needs most—an equality of commitment to know God and to obey his voice. The fact is, if she shares this commitment with her husband, or even, as my mother did for many years, holds it alone, she has the crucial ingredient for a fulfilling and joyous life.

Sisters in Christ, we must discipline ourselves to submit to God's will for our marriage relationships—to live as our husbands' helpers, submitting to and respecting their position, gracefully developing a gentle and quiet spirit. This is God's will in the gospel.

My parents' marriage was a far cry from the neat evangelical package I've described. Yet there was a genuineness and beauty in the promises made and kept by this laboring couple who faced what seemed like insurmountable odds. The result has been a harvest of grace, and I am part of it.

Kent and I have been married for forty-four years. We have four grown children and twenty-one grandchildren. Together we have tried to live out the directives of God's Word about marriage. Our struggles have been far different from those of my parents, and yet through them our commitment has grown, like my parents', into a deep and abiding love for each other. Our mutual commitment to live in accordance with God's plan for husband and wife has enabled us to experience a joyous unity—something rare and beautiful in this broken world.

My deepest regrets are for the times when I've failed the Lord by not being a respectful and submissive helper. My greatest joys have been the direct result of living in accordance with God's plan for me as a woman, made in his image—equal but different.

During the time that my husband and I worked to establish a biblical view of success, I sought to answer for myself, "What is my goal as a wife?" What I decided that day, thirty-one years ago, remains the same today: One day I want to hear God say to Kent, "Well done, good and faithful servant. Enter into the joy of your Master." As Kent's helper in this life, those words will be my joy. We will have ended well.

RENEW YOUR MIND

What expectations did you bring to marriage? How does the goal of holiness figure into your current expectations (see Eph. 5:22–31, esp. vv. 27–28)?

As a Christian, you must accept the authority of God and make it a life goal to submit every area of your life to his rule and order. What understanding do you glean from Genesis 1:26–28; 2:7, 18–25; 3:1–7, 14–17; and Ephesians 5:22–24 about God's order for authority in marriage? What does submission mean in specific terms for your marriage?

If you and your husband are "equal but different," why do you think God created an order for the marriage relationship? How does this order reflect the order in the Godhead?

How do you react, gut-level, at being termed your husband's "suitable helper"? How does understanding the role of Holy Spirit as "helper" dignify this role for you (see John 14:16)?

Why is gentleness countercultural for women in today's society?

Why is a woman's gentleness her true beauty (1 Pet. 3:3–6)? Who is the prime example for gentleness (Matt. 11:29)?

Why must you respect your husband whether or not he has earned your respect (see Eph. 5:33; 1 Pet. 3:6)? Take an inventory of your own recent actions and words. Do they show respect for your husband?

In view of the gospel, what are your personal goals as a wife?

LIBERATED THROUGH SUBMISSION

P. Bunny Wilson

AS WE WAITED FOR THE BEGINNING of the television interview, I focused on the woman seated next to me. We had chatted in the waiting room before the taping, and she struck me as a warm, sincere person. Her book was number ten on the *New York Times'* Bestseller List. Women were flocking to the stores to purchase this feminist's book, entitled *The Surrendered Wife*.[1]

Laura Doyle had become frustrated with the condition of her marriage; she began asking husbands what they wanted for their wives. To her surprise, most of them agreed they wanted to make their spouses happy. She concluded her husband had the same desires. So Laura decided she would stop nagging, complaining, and criticizing. She turned over all responsibilities to him (including the finances), she had sex with him anytime he wanted, and she gave him the choices of what movie they would see and which restaurant was best (along with every other decision). What happened? He became a fabulous husband, and she got what she wanted. Sincere? Yes. Surrendered? No.

The talk show host opened the program with the question, "What is the difference between surrender and submission?"

Laura stated her case for surrender and then expressed that she could never be submissive because that meant being beneath someone, being subservient and inferior. When the host turned to me with an inquisitive look, I replied, "If I defined submission as Laura just did, I would not want to do it either. Webster's Dictionary says submission means to 'yield to authority.' Submission is a powerful, positive, and aggressive principle intended for every man and woman, whether single or married. It should begin in our single life and extend into marriage."

The truth is, submission has gotten a bad rap because it has been defined improperly and applied incorrectly. It is usually the last place a woman will look to find peace and harmony for her life. The exciting part about Laura's book selling so well is that it signals that many women have come to the conclusion that what they've been doing is not working. They are looking for answers. However, when a woman decides to change the course of her life, she needs to consider the ramifications of the direction she chooses. She may see immediate results, as women have testified to experiencing through Laura's approach to marriage, but is she building her life and marriage on shifting sand?

Let's define *surrender*. Webster's Dictionary says it means "to give oneself up into the power of another." The fact is, the only one qualified to fill that position is God—first, because all power belongs to him, and second, because he won't abuse the power. The word *surrender* is a military term. It means a war is taking place, and someone wins and someone loses. Submission, on the other hand, is a win-win proposition.

If you should decide to read Laura's book, take a pen and circle the words *act*, *pretend*, and *imagine* each time they appear. Women are encouraged to go along with whatever their husbands want, not to "rock the boat," and then everything will be just fine. It doesn't matter that the wife feels or thinks differently; all that is required is that she act, pretend, and imagine. I remember those days when I acted out submission to my husband.

THE WEDDING GOWN

Years ago, while shopping in a mall near our home, I was drawn to a store window where an exquisite wedding gown was displayed.

The hustle and bustle of all the people around me seemed to cease. I could almost hear an imaginary organ playing the "Wedding March." My mind raced forward about twenty years, and I pictured my tiny daughter, Launi, gliding down a church aisle dressed in that lovely, white lace gown.

With a smile, I turned to the pretty, petite little girl at my side and lovingly said, "Just think, Launi, one day you'll wear a beautiful dress like that."

"I'm never getting married!" she fumed.

I was taken aback. How could a six-year-old make such a statement? How could *my* six-year-old make such a statement? My shocked reflection in the bridal shop window would have made Betty Friedan jump to her feet, shake her fist, and shout, "I told you so!"

As I tried to absorb the incident, I thought perhaps Launi was just a little overtired from our long walk through the mall. But a second look at her quietly determined face told me she had given her outburst a considerable amount of thought.

My mind raced backwards to my own childhood when I, too, had come to some definite conclusions relating to marriage. Until meeting my husband, I had been a confirmed bachelorette who didn't want to ever get married or have children. Once I met Frank, however, I discovered some qualities in him I had not seen in any other man. I decided to take the plunge.

Now, fighting to regain my composure, I asked Launi to repeat what she had said. I was hoping she'd mixed up a few words. Fixing her eyes on mine, she firmly repeated, "I'm *never* getting married!"

Naturally, my next question was, "Why?"

Launi's response altered the course of my "submissive" life!

"Because I'm not going to have a man tell me what to do like Daddy tells you what to do. You have to ask him to do everything! You don't like it, and I won't either!"

I was reduced to a stammering, stuttering defense. "I don't ask Daddy everything," I insisted. "Why, I came to the mall today all by myself, and I didn't even ask him!"

The disgusted expression on her face was enough to tell me my portrait should hang in the Hall of Hypocrites.

So this was the result of all my dutiful submission. I should have known it wouldn't work. This six-year-old had seen right through all my smiles and surrendering. I felt as if I had been living in a dark cave for years and had suddenly been jerked out into the startling sunlight.

For six years I had been determined to carry out the act of submission, and now I was reaping the consequences. I began to ask God for a correct understanding and application of the principle of submission. Once I learned it, I was amazed at its liberating power.

ON THE AIR

It's important we understand submission in its entirety. Remember my interview with Laura Doyle? The interviewer asked me if submission was only for people who believe in the Bible. I responded that submission is not only a Christian principle, but it is a universal principle. Then I shared the following example.

One day I was interviewed on a secular radio station about my book on submission. Bob, the talk show host, informed me they had advertised the program heavily. There were a lot of people waiting for the phone lines to open up.

Once Bob introduced me, he immediately jumped in with the statement, "So, Bunny, you've come on the air today to teach wives they must submit to their husbands."

Amused, I replied, "No, Bob, I'm here today to share that you're a submitted man."

"How so?" he asked.

"Well, Webster's Dictionary defines the word submit as 'to yield,' which is voluntary. Do you own this radio station?"

"No."

"Do you have a general manager?"

"Yes."

"Do you always agree with the programming assigned to you?"

"Of course not."

"Then the very fact I'm speaking to you today means you are a submitted man."

Bob burst into laughter and replied, "I guess you're right!"

After we had conversed for a short time on the subject, he opened up the telephone lines. The first caller, Harriet, who had obviously been waiting for this moment, announced emphatically, "Hello, Bunny Bimbo! They need to take your book and burn it in a fire!"

Refusing to be disturbed by her outburst, I asked her how she defined submission. She equated it with subservience, physical abuse, and being asked to do something immoral. I explained that submission has gotten a bad name because it has been defined incorrectly and applied improperly.

Then I inquired, "Did you know feminists are submitted women?"

Harriet sounded as if she was gnawing on the telephone, but I continued, "Many feminist groups have an organizational flowchart. When the board meets to make decisions for their organization, they may disagree, but everyone knows the president has the right to make the final decision. Before they leave that room, those in disagreement must *graciously submit* because they know a 'house divided against itself cannot stand.'"

The reality is, everyone submits to something. It's never a question of, "Do you submit?" but rather, "To what or whom are you submitted?" As believers, it is imperative that we accept God's Word as our organizational flowchart, whether we are male or female, single or married. As you learn more about the liberating principle of submission and apply it to your life, you'll discover that submission really means "God intervenes."

THE BROKEN TRAFFIC SIGNAL

In my book for singles who would one day like to be married, *Knight in Shining Armor*, I give an example that bears repeating. It helps illustrate the simplicity of the powerful principle of submission.

Before you drive your car to a destination, you probably don't pray, "Lord, whatever you do, please don't let there be a broken traffic signal at a busy intersection on the way or I'll never get to where I'm going!"

Why don't we pray that prayer? Because we know that when we come to an intersection and the traffic signal is broken, there is an established procedure that allows traffic to proceed smoothly. The first thing we do is stop. We allow the cars on the right to proceed first. After they go, the process is continued until the traffic signal is repaired. Now what if an order had not been established? There would be utter chaos in the intersection, and people would be arguing and bumping into each other, trying to prove they have the right of way.

Have you ever wondered why we need the principle of submission? Submission in earthly relationships provides a beautiful picture of the relationships within the Trinity and of God's redemptive plan. But another practical explanation is that God knew he had created free-thinking individuals and that by nature every person does what is right in his own eyes. He also knew that if any two people spent any amount of time together, sooner or later their communication would collapse—the "signal" would be broken. If an order had not been established, there would be utter confusion in the relationship.

Unfortunately, there are many believers who do not understand the principle of submission, and their relationships are filled with anger and chaos. However, as we all know, ignorance of the law does not excuse us from the penalty of the law. Whether married or single, male or female, we are required to submit to God (James 4:7), to the spiritual leadership of the church (Heb. 13:17), to employers (1 Pet. 2:18), and to the government (1 Pet. 2:13–14). The practice of submission in single life will directly affect the success of submission in married life.

In the marriage relationship the wife is not the only one who is called to submit. The husband is to yield to God by loving his wife "as Christ loved the church" (Eph. 5:25), by being the final decision-maker (Eph. 5:22), by being the spiritual head (Eph. 5:26), and by living with her "in an understanding way" (1 Pet. 3:7). The wife is called to submit to her husband's final decisions (Eph. 5:22).

Let's look at this principle of submission in the context of the workplace. Suppose your employer gives you an assignment with which you do not agree. You feel strongly that his or her idea is a waste of time. Do you go to the lunchroom and complain to your colleagues about your boss's decision? If you do, you violate the Word of God, which says:

> Do all things without grumbling or questioning, that you may be blameless and innocent, children of God without blemish in the midst of a

crooked and twisted generation, among whom you shine as lights in the world. (Phil. 2:14–15)

According to that Scripture, there should never be complaining or arguing among believers. Does that mean we are supposed to let people walk over us? No; the proper procedure works just like when there is a broken traffic signal.

When your boss makes what you view as an unreasonable request, the first thing you should do is stop. You need time to collect your thoughts and keep yourself from reacting emotionally and saying or doing something foolish.

The next step is to *speak the truth*. You may think, "Well, that won't be hard!" It may be harder than you think if it's done according to Ephesians 4:15, where God's Word says we are to "speak the truth in love." I was fired from three jobs because I spoke the truth in anger and frustration. When we share the truth in love we will speak honestly, with the right tone of voice, facial expression, and gestures. If your employer does not agree with you, the next step is to submit (yield) and give the issue to God.

Submission is such a powerful principle because it operates on faith, and "without faith it is impossible to please [God]" (Heb. 11:6).

It takes faith to believe that God knows all and hears all and will intervene on our behalf without any further input from us. In the situation with your employer, it means you believe the Lord can communicate into his heart and mind (whether or not he is a believer) and is able to lead him in the right direction.

THE FINAL VERDICT

After Jesus died on the cross for our sins, God could have written in his Word, "If you confess with your mouth and believe in your heart that God raised him from the dead, you will be saved . . . The End." God could have left us here to deal with life and the Devil on our own and just waited patiently until we died and went to heaven. The fact that he cares about every aspect of our lives between here and heaven is an incredible blessing. However, if we want to reap the reward, we have to allow him to intervene. Remember: *submission means God intervenes.*

For those of us who are married, sharing the truth in love will allow God to use us as an effective "helper" in our husband's life (see Gen. 2:18). Many married women attempt to sweep controversial issues under the rug in the name of peace. That just puts lumps in the carpet, and after a while neither spouse is able to walk through the relationship without tripping.

The last step is to *wait* on God to demonstrate what his will is concerning the situation. The goal is not to prove who is right and who is wrong but to discover the will of God on the matter. Sometimes we have all the facts correct, but the conclusion still is not his will.

Remember the illustration of dealing with the employer? His imagination will be staggered when with a cheerful heart and attitude you tackle a project to which he knows you are personally opposed. Your gracious demeanor will speak volumes about your relationship with the Lord.

But what if your employer—or pastor or husband—makes a decision that is clearly a poor one? The real question is not if but when. No one is perfect, and mistakes are inevitable. However, when we operate according to the principle of submission, mistakes become blessings. Faith recognizes that God can make a straight line with a crooked stick.

Mistakes on the part of those in authority are our opportunity to say, "Because I am a Christian, I submit to your decision. I believe God can lead you in the way you should go. I also believe if you make a mistake, God can fix it. Now what can I do to help?"

When people who are in authority in our lives make a mistake and we are there to help them fix it, that expression of kindness allows them to accept what they did as being wrong instead of needing to justify or blame. It endears them to us, and the light of Jesus Christ is clearly seen in us. The next time we give our opinion, we can be sure they will give it greater consideration because we will have earned the right to be heard.

TOUCHÉ

One of the greatest blessings of practicing submission has been seeing it emulated in my children. When my daughter, Launi, was planning her wedding to the wonderful young man who is now my son-in-law,

I made her agree she would faithfully send out thank you notes for the gifts they received. She promised to be diligent in that area, knowing it was important to me.

Months after the ceremony a few of our relatives and friends started questioning me as to whether Launi had received their gift. I was upset—I couldn't dial her number fast enough. When I confronted her with her obvious lack of diligence she responded, "I'm sorry, Mom, but Jason said he wanted me to wait until he had time to sit down with me and do it together. So in submission to my husband, I have waited."

There was silence on my end. She got me; that's what I had taught her for years. Smiling, I encouraged her to remind her husband it was important to follow through on the thank you notes and hung up the telephone. I rejoiced in knowing she understood and was practicing submission.

PATIENCE

Patience is one of the main ingredients necessary for a successful submitted life. Yet it is something that is sorely lacking in most of our lives, because it requires us to release control of a situation. We must walk in faith, believing that God will intervene when we are called to submit to someone in authority.

Time and time again I have counseled with women who desire to come home and raise their children but whose husbands insist on their working outside the home. They wake up early and rush to get the children ready to drop off at day care or school. Then they spend eight hours at work, finishing just in time to pick up the children from school; or worse, their children come home to an empty house while they are still at work. Once they get home, there is dinner to fix, homework to help with, baths to take, and bedtime rituals. And let's not forget about the house or apartment that needs attention. And unfortunately, too many times there is little assistance from the spouse.

I can't count the number of women who have sat across from me in my living room and cried because they just couldn't seem to get their husbands to understand how difficult it is for them to have to work outside the home. Many of these stressed-out women have

133

been surprised to hear me say, "You must submit to your husband's decision."

Let me quickly say I have never seen one case where a woman heeded that counsel and ended up remaining in the workplace. But it is important for her to do this God's way—to yield to her husband's authority and then get out of God's way.

Scripture teaches that God's plan is for wives to be "keepers at home" (Titus 2:5, KJV), and it's difficult to do that without being at home. But the Lord resists us when we do things out of order. Even in scenarios where women are the sole provider for their children, God will show himself strong on behalf of the mother if she gives him time and exercises patience.

When my sister-in-law, Audree, gave her heart to the Lord, she hit the ground running. I don't think I've ever met anyone who has equaled her passion for God as a new believer. She grasped quickly the importance of being a "keeper at home" and shared with my brother, Cliff, her desire to leave the workplace. The challenge was that her income equaled his, and they needed both incomes just to make ends meet. However, she believed God would provide, and Cliff consented. Within a week he was promoted in his job and began making twice as much.

At the beginning of 1999, I started mentoring eight young wives. Two of them had small children and were working outside the home. Both expressed that there was no way their husbands would allow them to quit their jobs. Both heeded my advice to stay under their husband's authority. Before the year ended, they were both out of the workforce and back at home.

While having dinner at our home, one of the women's husbands made a profound observation. He said, "I remember the day my wife turned me over to the Lord. She didn't tell me that's what she had done, but I knew it had taken place. Before, when she would contend with me, it allowed me to justify decisions I knew were not pleasing to the Lord. But when she relinquished control, the only person I had to deal with was the Lord, and that's an uncomfortable position."

Patience is the key. Once those wives released the situation into the Lord's hand, they experienced peace, even before the situation was resolved. Just knowing they were praying in God's will and that in due season he would intervene delivered them from stress.

A wise person once said, "You don't break God's laws; they break you!" If the word *submission* makes the hair stand up on the back of your neck, that suggests you are a victim of the wrong definition and application of this liberating principle. Don't let the world steal from you the joy of walking in obedience to God in this area. Submission is the pathway he has designed to provide the greatest possible freedom and blessing for every believer. Stand by and watch him intervene on your behalf when you do things "decently and in order" (1 Cor. 14:40).

HOW TO RAISE
FEMININE DAUGHTERS

Susan Hunt

THE VERY FACT THAT WE are asking how to bequeath femininity to our daughters is a sign of the times. We live in a postmodern, relativistic culture that has so thoroughly lost its way that even the simple issue of girls naturally maturing into womanhood is mired in confusion. So how do we approach this topic?

The dictionary defines *feminine* as "belonging to the female sex; characterized by or possessing qualities generally attributed to a woman; womanly."

I could seize that definition and inject it full of the qualities I think should "generally [be] attributed to a woman." I could write a treatise on the obvious effects of feminism and issue a call to women to return to traditional values. I could give a checklist of what good Christian mothers and fathers should be sure their daughters do and don't do. And believe me, I do have opinions! However, a formulaic, prescriptive, behavioral approach is like shifting sand. It may give immediate ideas and temporary solutions, but it will not challenge our daughters to make lasting commitments and changes in the depths of their hearts.

Any discussion of femininity must be driven by God's Word or it will lack substance, integrity, and longevity. I am fully aware of the volatility of this topic, but my primary concern is to present a biblical foundation for womanhood. I believe this positive approach will help us show and tell our daughters the wonders of God's design and calling for women.

One sidebar before we explore this topic: as we think about raising feminine daughters, I encourage you to think covenantally and not just biologically. Our salvation is personal and individual; but when God saves us, he adopts us into his covenant family. We have spiritual brothers, sisters, mothers, and daughters. God deals with us as a household of faith. Whether or not we have biological daughters, we have spiritual daughters, and it is our covenant privilege and responsibility to pass on a legacy of biblical womanhood to those girls and young women entrusted to our church.

Now let's explore a biblical foundation for womanhood.

PURPOSE AND AUTHORITY

Whenever we craft a biblical apologetic for any topic, we need to begin by putting that topic in the larger context of creation, fall, and redemption. If we simply lift a few Scripture verses out of context and use those verses to construct our apologetic, we will likely come away with distortions. The same is true for womanhood. Our starting point is not roles and behaviors. The fundamental question is: What is our purpose and authority? Creation, fall, and redemption give the answers.

The opening words of Scripture tell us that "In the beginning God created the heavens and the earth. . . . God said, 'Let there be light,' and there was light" (Gen. 1:1, 3).

God is the Creator. He spoke, and creation happened. His Word is the absolute authority.

On the sixth day of creation God said, "Let us make man in our image, after our likeness. And let them have dominion over the fish of the sea and over the birds of the heavens and over the livestock and over all the earth and over every creeping thing that creeps on the earth" (Gen. 1:26).

It is incredible that the God whose words brought creation into existence would make a creature in his own image. The Creator King fashioned a creature that would mirror certain aspects of his own character. This is what would set this creature apart from all the others.

So God created man in his own image, in the image of God he created him; male and female he created them. (Gen. 1:27)

The man and the woman were created with the capacity to reflect the very character of God. Herein lies the purpose and dignity of humankind.

Purpose and authority are the first steps in building a biblical worldview, including our perspective of womanhood. *The Westminster Shorter Catechism* underscores this by beginning with these two foundational questions:

Q. 1. What is the chief end of man?
A. Man's chief end is to glorify God and to enjoy Him forever.
Q. 2. What rule hath God given to direct us how we may glorify and enjoy Him?
A. The word of God, which is contained in the Scriptures of the Old and New Testaments, is the only rule to direct us how we may glorify and enjoy Him.[1]

Our purpose is God's glory, and our authority to know how to glorify him is his Word. This shapes and simplifies life.

But the first man and woman rebelled against God's authority. Adam and Eve chose self-governance rather than God's rule. Sin separated them from God and from the reason for their existence. They could no longer live in God's presence, and so they could no longer reflect his glory. Adam was our representative; so his fallen nature and the wretched consequences of his sin were passed on to the human race.

But God did not leave us in this predicament. Through the covenant of grace, God made the way for us to be redeemed from sin and to live in his presence. In this covenant, Christ is our representative. He kept the terms of the covenant for us. He lived a perfectly obedient life and offered himself as the payment for our sin. God's covenant promise is, "I will give them a heart to know that I am the LORD, and they shall be my people and I will be their God, for they shall return to me with their whole heart" (Jer. 24:7). We do not deserve salvation, and we can do nothing to earn it. It is glorious grace from beginning to end.

SOME PRACTICAL IMPLICATIONS OF
PURPOSE AND AUTHORITY

Our daughters will be products of their theology. Their knowledge—or lack of knowledge—of who God is and what he has done for them will show up in every attitude, action, and relationship. Their worldview will be determined by their belief system.

We must teach our daughters that their value and identity lie in the fact that they are image bearers of the God of glory. This will protect them from seeking significance in the inconsequential shallowness of self-fulfillment, personal happiness, materialism, or others' approval.

Our daughters must know the wondrous truth that their overarching purpose in life is God's glory. This must determine every decision they make, from their choice of clothes to their choice of a husband. The question that guides all of our decisions should be: Does this glorify God? First Corinthians 10:31 should be one of the first verses they memorize: "So, whether you eat or drink, or whatever you do, do all to the glory of God." And they should see us making decisions based on this mandate.

The world will tempt our daughters to look to their feelings and experiences as their authority, but we must show and tell them that God's Word is the ultimate authority for faith and life.

We must tell our daughters about the expanse of God's love. They must know that we are justified and sanctified by grace. It seems that women are particularly prone to a performance orientation of life. We may acknowledge that we are saved by grace, but somehow we get entangled in "works righteousness" when it comes to our sanctification. We think that if we are a little better, God will love us a little more. This distortion spills over into all other relationships. *If I'm a little better, my parents will love me more* . . . or *my friends will love me more* . . . or *my husband will love me more*. This is exhausting for the one trying to earn everyone's love, and it drains the people whose approval we are trying to earn. Children who think they must establish their own righteousness through accepted behavior eventually become so weary that they give up or become masters of deceit.

A biblical understanding of justification will free our daughters. The more they understand that God declares us to be just in his sight on the basis of the finished work of Jesus Christ and that the righteousness of Jesus is deposited in our spiritual bank accounts, the more they will live in the beauty and freedom of his grace.

All of this means that I must search my own heart. Am I trying to elevate myself through my daughter's accomplishments and behavior? Is my primary concern her happiness or her holiness? Is God's glory really the driving passion of my own life? These questions take me to the cross. They take me to Jesus to plead for grace and wisdom.

It is against this backdrop that we are able to perceive the particular uniqueness of God's creation of woman.

WOMAN'S CREATION DESIGN

In Genesis 2 we read, "The LORD God said, 'It is not good that the man should be alone; I will make him a helper fit for him'" (v. 18).

Why was it "not good that the man should be alone"? Because he was created in the image of the Triune God. The unity and diversity of the Trinity demanded an image bearer that reflected this equal but different characteristic.

Equality did not preclude gender distinctiveness; rather, equality allowed the distinctiveness of the man and the woman to be so perfectly complementary that it blended into a mysterious oneness that gloriously reflected the oneness of the Trinity.

The helper design of the woman brought a completeness to the garden home that received God's pronouncement, "It is very good."

Yet we live in a culture whose hostility against this design and order has raged for several decades. The feminist philosophy says that equality means sameness and insists on independence from husbands and family. Now the daughters of those feminists are confused.

In her book *What Our Mothers Didn't Tell Us*, Danielle Crittenden writes:

> For in all the ripping down of barriers that has taken place over a generation, we may have inadvertently also smashed the foundations necessary for our happiness. Pretending that we are the same as men—with similar needs and desires—has only led many of us to find out, brutally, how different we really are. In demanding radical independence—from men, from our families—we may have also abandoned certain bargains and institutions that didn't always work

perfectly but until very recently were civilization's best ways of taming the feckless human heart.[2]

Mrs. Crittenden's research and analysis are helpful, but her solutions are flawed because they begin with woman and not with God. She, too, is searching for what will make women happy, and it is an endless journey.

I pray that our daughters will write books entitled *What Our Mothers Told Us* and that these books will celebrate God's creation purpose and his design of woman. This is a design that is never outdated because it transcends time and place. It is bigger than any given role in life, but it impacts every role. It is the design stamped upon us at creation. It is intrinsic to who we are as women.

So, let's explore this helper design. In the Old Testament the Hebrew word for *helper* is used primarily to refer to God as our Helper. When we consider how God is our Helper, we begin to see the richness and strength of this word.

Moses spoke of God as his Helper who saved him from the sword of Pharaoh (Ex. 18:4).

In Psalms we read that God is the Helper of the victim, the fatherless, the needy, and the afflicted (Ps. 10:14; 72:12; 86:17).

God is referred to as our Helper who is our support, strength, and shield (Ps. 20:2; 28:7; 33:20).

I think you get the picture. This is not a fragile word, and we are not called to a mission of fluff. Our helper ministry is one of defense, comfort, and compassion. I addressed this topic in my book *By Design*:

> The helper design is multi-dimensional. Different women will exhibit different aspects of this design in various ways. The same woman may exhibit it differently in each season of her life. . . . The relational strength of our helper design causes women to attach fiercely to people and purposes. We don't turn loose easily. This tenacity equips women to persevere in intercessory prayer for years. Countless mothers have prayed for wayward children long after others lost hope. . . .
>
> We live in a culture void of hope. Woman's helper design uniquely qualifies us to enter this vacuum and to give help by proclaiming the "Hope of Israel, its Savior in times of distress" (Jer. 14:8).
>
> In Psalm 146, the words *help* (ezer) and *hope* are linked together.

This is significant. Help apart from hope is superficial and temporary. It is merely a stopgap measure that is a substitute for the real thing. Yet this is what our culture offers. . . .

The woman who can give authentic help is the one who has come to a place of hopelessness in self that drives her to God's Word where she finds her "help is the God of Jacob," and her "hope is in the Lord." She is qualified to help others because she has an eternal relationship with the Lord and she is saturated with His Word. She points them to the only viable Object of hope by directing them to the only veritable Source of hope. This is authentic help.[3]

Sin marred that design, and now woman tries to reinvent womanhood on her own terms. Since Satan slithered into the garden and convinced Eve to try the way of independence and individualism, women have been on a quest for their own happiness. In this autonomous vacuum the helper design is senseless and useless.

It is because of our redemption that we *can* live out our helper design. It is our redemption that breaks the reign of sin in our lives and empowers us to fulfill our creation mission. And it is our knowledge of our Redeemer's love for us that compels us to do so. In the covenant community, the helper design makes sense. Two of the characteristics of covenant life are community and compassion, and this is exactly what our helper design equips us to cultivate. Our nurturing and relational strengths prepare us to foster a sense of family in the home and church and to be channels of compassion to the victims, fatherless, needy, and afflicted.

SOME PRACTICAL IMPLICATIONS OF THE HELPER DESIGN

The redeemed woman who has a biblical apologetic of womanhood has a focus and clarity of purpose that enables her to be a true helper. She will embrace her helper design and will encourage and equip her daughters to do the same.

The redeemed helper will be a woman of prayer. She will defend her family and the covenant family on her knees, and her daughters will be drawn to emulate her selfless strength.

The redeemed helper whose covenant sensibilities have been honed understands the importance of the virtue of domesticity and the ministry of hospitality. But she knows this is more than baking her own bread and having a beautifully decorated home. Domesticity means a devotion to home life. It seems to me that the most definitive statement of domesticity was made by Jesus when he said, "Let not your hearts be troubled. . . . In my Father's house are many rooms. If it were not so, would I have told you that I go to prepare a place for you?" (John 14:1–2).

Domesticity means that we prepare safe places where troubled hearts can find rest and comfort, and we involve our daughters in this ministry in our homes and in our churches. In a must-read book for every woman, nineteenth-century pastor John Angell James said, "Whatever breaks down the modest reserve, the domestic virtues, the persuasive gentleness, of woman, is an injury done to the community."[4]

The redeemed helper is not inward-focused. You will find her taking her children to visit the elderly as well as taking them across social and cultural barriers to extend the boundaries of the covenant to the oppressed and needy and afflicted. And as she does so, she trains another generation to live covenantally.

The redeemed helper who is not married understands that she is to be a mother in Israel and that she is to join with other women to be corporate helpers in God's covenant community.

The redeemed helper values male and female distinctiveness because she knows that this is God's design and order. She is not threatened by male headship. She knows that submission has nothing to do with status. Submission has to do with function. It is the way God has ordered life in the kingdom, and it is good because he is good. This is a reflection of the ontological equality yet the functional difference in the Trinity. Headship and submission are God's ordained means for achieving oneness in marriage. She knows that submission is not a legalistic list of behaviors or mindless passivity. She understands that it is not about logic; it is about love. It defies logic that Jesus would release all the glories of heaven so that he could give us the glory of heaven. In Philippians we are told:

> Have this mind among yourselves, which is yours in Christ Jesus, who, though he was in the form of God, did not count equality with God a thing to be grasped, but made himself nothing, taking the form of a servant, being born in the likeness of men. And being found in human

form, he humbled himself by becoming obedient to the point of death, even death on a cross. (Phil. 2:5–8)

Jesus loved us so much that he voluntarily submitted to death on a cross. His command is that wives are to submit to their husbands. This is a gift that we voluntarily give to the man we have vowed to love, in obedience to the Savior we love. The redeemed helper knows that submission does not restrict her—it actually frees her to fulfill her helper design. And as she lives in the light of this truth, her daughters watch and learn.

> There is an interesting verse in Psalm 144: ". . . our daughters like corner pillars cut for the structure of a palace" (v. 12).
>
> A pillar, according to the dictionary, is "a . . . support; one who occupies a central or responsible position." Some of the meanings of the root Hebrew word that is used here are: "to attend, to defend, to give stability, to join." The ideas of protection and support are clear in this imagery.
>
> In summary, a helper supports by protecting, sustaining, upholding, refreshing, attending, defending, and stabilizing.[5]

HOW DO WE PASS THE LEGACY OF BIBLICAL WOMANHOOD TO OUR DAUGHTERS?

This is certainly not an exhaustive list of suggestions, but at least it will get us started.

First, we must remember that God has given us every resource we need. He has given us his Holy Spirit. We have the very power of God within us to give us grace and wisdom for the task, and we must pray for this same power to be at work in our daughters. It is the power of the gospel that will transform them.

> For I am not ashamed of the gospel, for it is the power of God for salvation to everyone who believes, to the Jew first and also to the Greek. (Rom. 1:16)

> And we all, with unveiled face, beholding the glory of the Lord, are being transformed into the same image from one degree of glory to another. For this comes from the Lord who is the Spirit. (2 Cor. 3:18)

He has given us his Word. We must diligently teach our daughters biblical truth and pray that the Holy Spirit will apply that truth to their hearts.

How can a young man [or woman] keep his [or her] way pure? By guarding it according to your word. . . . I have stored up your word in my heart, that I might not sin against you. (Ps. 119:9, 11)

He has given us the privilege of prayer. We should pray for hedges of protection around our daughters. Select portions of Scripture, and pray them into your daughter's life. For example, pray that she will trust in the Lord with all her heart and never lean on her own understanding; that in all her ways she will acknowledge him, for he will make her paths straight. Pray that she will not be wise in her own eyes, but that she will fear the Lord and shun evil (see Prov. 3:5–7). Pray Proverbs 31 for her.

The Lord has given us the church. The covenant family is part of our inheritance as members of the family of God. The church is "a pillar and buttress of the truth" (1 Tim. 3:15), and believing parents have the unrivaled resource of the teaching and the relationships provided there. Louis Berkhof wrote:

Now, the children of the covenant are adopted into a family that is infinitely higher than the family of any man of rank or nobility. They are adopted into the family of the covenant God himself. Even while on earth they are privileged to join the company of the redeemed, the saints of God. They take their place in the church of Jesus Christ, which is the heavenly Jerusalem.[6]

When our daughters are taught the truth of biblical womanhood, and they see the wonder and substance of this reality being lived out among Christian women, I believe they will be dazzled and will flourish.

The righteous flourish like the palm tree
and grow like a cedar in Lebanon.
They are planted in the house of the LORD;
they flourish in the courts of our God.

They still bear fruit in old age;
   they are ever full of sap and green,
to declare that the LORD is upright;
   he is my rock, and there is no unrighteousness in him.
   (Ps. 92:12–15)

Second, the fight to recapture biblical womanhood is a spiritual battle, and we must utilize every weapon God has provided as we engage in this conflict. We cannot deny the fact that we have breathed feminist air for several decades. This poison has taken its toll. Raising daughters who are committed to a biblical perspective of womanhood will be like standing against a tidal wave. But stand we must.

Finally, be strong in the Lord and in the strength of his might. Put on the whole armor of God, that you may be able to stand against the schemes of the devil. For we do not wrestle against flesh and blood, but against the rulers, against the authorities, against the cosmic powers over this present darkness, against the spiritual forces of evil in the heavenly places. Therefore take up the whole armor of God, that you may be able to withstand in the evil day, and having done all, to stand firm. (Eph. 6:10–13)

Third, we must teach our daughters that living for God's glory is beyond their ability. It is a work of grace. We should teach them to flee to the cross for grace and mercy, and then to become a stream of grace and mercy to others. They will learn this best by seeing us live in this way.

Fourth, we must teach our daughters about biblical womanhood as we "sit in our house and when [we] walk by the way, and when [we] lie down and when [we] rise" (Deut. 6:7). We are teaching a way of life as we live life.

John Angell James, the nineteenth-century pastor quoted earlier, wrote about teaching our children through the course of everyday circumstances:

It is the sentiments you let drop occasionally, it is the conversation they overhear, when playing in the corner of the room, which has more effect than many things which are addressed to them directly. . . . Your example will educate them—your conversation with your friends—the business they see you transact—the likings and dislikings you express—these will educate them . . . the education of circumstances. . . . is of more constant and powerful effect, and of far more consequence to the habit, than that which is direct and apparent. This education goes on at every instant of time; it goes on like time—you can neither stop it nor turn its course.[7]

Fifth, we must not be naïve. We must be wise, like the men of Issachar, "who had understanding of the times, to know what Israel ought to do, 200 chiefs, and all their kinsmen under their command" (1 Chron. 12:32). We must be aware of cultural influences, and we must warn our daughters of the dangers of ungodliness.

What kind of women will it take to raise feminine daughters? It will take true women.

THE TRUE WOMAN

In a book by this title I give the following explanation:

The dictionary defines *true* as "consistent with fact or reality; exactly conforming to a rule, standard, or pattern." . . .

The true woman is the real thing. She is a genuine, authentic Masterpiece. The Master has set eternity in her heart and is conforming her to His own image. There is consistency in her outward behavior because it is dictated by the reality of her inner life. That reality is her redemption.

The true woman is a reflection of her redemption. . . . By the transforming power of the Gospel, the Christian woman is empowered by God's Spirit to give an increasingly true reflection of her Savior and thus to be a true woman. . . .

When my friend Sharon Kraemer was diagnosed with cancer, her response was, "I am confident that God will use this to take me deeper into His love for me." I didn't see Sharon until several weeks after surgery and several rounds of chemotherapy, and at my first sight of her I gasped. It was not because her body and her hair were so thin. My shock was because Sharon absolutely glowed with peace and love. She was awash with an undeniable radiance. I could only exclaim, "Sharon, you must have been spending some incredible times with the Lord." She did not need to reply. The evidence was there.

This is the essence of the true woman. Regardless of the time in history when she inhabits this earth, she is one who lives in the presence of glory. Her redeemed character is shaped and driven by God's Word and Spirit. Because she is the very dwelling-place of the Lord God, her reflection of Him is manifested in every relationship and circumstance of life. The distinguishing characteristic of her life is His presence in her radiating out to all who see her. The true woman's life is not segmented into sacred and secular. All of life is sacred because it is lived in His presence. The true woman is a true reflection of God's glory.[8]

Recently our granddaughter, Mary Kate, made her public profession of faith and was received as a full communing member of her church. Three generations of women in our family sat together and watched the fourth generation pledge herself to Jesus Christ as each of us had done. There was a rush of gratitude for God's covenant faithfulness to families, and a profound sense of our responsibility to pass on a legacy of biblical womanhood. Mary Kate, and the generation of covenant daughters she represents, does not foresee the battles to be fought. But, to some degree, we know. And we are covenant-bound to "so train the young women. . . . Show yourself in all respects to be a model of good works . . . waiting for our blessed hope, the appearing of the glory of our great God and Savior Jesus Christ, who gave himself for us to redeem us from all lawlessness and to purify for himself a people for his own possession who are zealous for good works" (Titus 2:4, 7, 13–14).

May God give us grace and wisdom, and may he be pleased to give us daughters who have a passion to live for and to reflect his glory.

NURTURING MOTHERS

Dorothy Kelley Patterson

IF YOU ARE A WOMAN, whether you are married or single and whether or not you have physical children, there is a maternal spirit within your very nature. That maternal instinct has been given to you by God himself and is an essential part of his plan for reproducing his heart in the next generation.

At times a woman may consider maternity as excess baggage—something that interferes with her life, her career, or her ministry. A woman's maternal spirit needs to be sanctified by the Lord to be available to be used whenever, wherever, and however he chooses. Let me share a vignette from my own life to illustrate this process of surrender.

Paige Patterson and I married while we were both students at Hardin-Simmons University. At the time I was immersed in Greek studies, and it never occurred to me that I might become pregnant in the midst of the awesome task of preparing myself to translate the Greek New Testament. My Greek professor had announced in our first class that we were required to be present every day in order to pass the course.

When I became pregnant halfway through the semester, the thought passed through my mind, *Lord, You know I'm in this Greek class, not to mention other challenging studies. I am planning to complete my studies in a year. Is this timing really appropriate?*

Within a few weeks and without any warning, I began the process of miscarrying that baby. I immediately went to complete bed rest in an effort to save the life that was forming in my womb. My husband brought home my class work and helped me keep up. My Greek professor even came to our house to help me with the language study, but my focus was on trying to protect that life in my womb. My university studies had suddenly paled in importance.

Looking back on that time, I believe the Lord wanted to get my attention. For reasons known only to him, I lost that baby while in great pain, alone in my home. I went through a period of great discouragement and anguish. Suddenly my entire focus was on maternity. I couldn't have cared less about my Greek studies or any aspect of my formal education.

Some months after my miscarriage, in a regular checkup, the doctor discovered a growth in my reproductive system. At the time there wasn't a simple way to find out whether this cyst was benign or cancerous. The doctor elected to watch it carefully. Within months the cyst began growing rapidly, entwining itself around my ovaries so that within a year I was facing major surgery. The doctor held little hope that he could save my ovaries, and I had to sign a form acknowledging that I was giving up my fertility. I went into that surgery with many fears and little hope. The doctor had to remove part of both ovaries. Although he could not give me any encouragement, I clung to the hope that I would not be infertile and barren. More than ever I yearned for the opportunity to bear and nurture a child.

Some years later I became pregnant again. This time I carried the baby to full term. I went into labor on a Saturday evening. Everything seemed to be going well. The next morning, while I was still in labor, my doctor said, "I'm going to take my offering envelope down to the church, and I'll be right back." In the brief time it took him to walk two blocks to the church and back to the hospital, the baby in my womb had managed to jerk his umbilical cord loose. Suddenly he was without oxygen. When the doctor discovered what had happened, he hurriedly sought my husband to deliver the bleak message that the baby would be dead. He asked Paige for permission to send me to surgery with the understanding that the baby was lost.

Paige knew me well enough to respond quickly and firmly, "Doctor, you get her into surgery as fast as you can. You do your best job to save our baby, and let's leave this in God's hands." God was gracious indeed because he gave Paige and me a wonderful son who was perfectly healthy despite the fact that he had been without oxygen for the fourteen minutes it took to move me into surgery, make the incision, and deliver him. That precious son—Armour Paige Patterson—was entrusted to us to rear in the Lord. God had again taught me a valuable lesson for the ministry I was going to have with women. Women have to learn and then be reminded again and again of the value of life and of our unique calling to be life givers.

Several years later again I was given the opportunity to nurture life when God blessed us with a daughter. The doctor elected to take the baby early because a C-section was necessary. However, he miscalculated the due date; instead of taking the baby two weeks early, he took her a month early. As a result, the baby contracted Hylane Membrane Disease. Within hours of her delivery, the doctor came to tell me that my baby girl was critically ill and was not going to live. The only neonatal center at that time was in New York City, and our tiny daughter was too weak to be moved. She was born on Friday; and on Sunday night while God's people all across the United States were praying, God touched that darling girl. You would love our beautiful Carmen, who is now the mother of our two granddaughters. How thankful I am that God gave this infertile, barren woman—me—a woman who failed her first test—another chance to be a bearer and nurturer of life.

The maternity God placed in my nature, however, has not been directed just to our biological children, though they are definitely at the top of the list. Over the years God has brought many young people to my living room sofa and to my kitchen table, where I have had the opportunity to pour into their lives the love and nurture that God himself placed in my heart.

Often I remind women that the nurturing experiences God has for us do not always come in a preconceived pattern. You do not have to have a biological child born into your home; you are not limited to a certain season of time. You must be willing and ready to use your maternity as God sees fit. If you are, I think you will be as excited as I have been to link hands with the Creator God in creating and nurturing life. There is no higher calling!

A BIBLICAL ROLE MODEL

The Old Testament introduces a wonderful role model. Her story gives us a number of insights into what it means to have a nurturing mother's heart. The opening verses of the book of 1 Samuel provide the backdrop:

> There was a certain man of Ramathaim-zophim of the hill country of Ephraim whose name was Elkanah. . . . He had two wives. The name of the one was Hannah, and the name of the other, Peninnah. And Peninnah had children, but Hannah had no children.
>
> Now this man used to go up year by year from his city to worship and to sacrifice to the LORD of hosts at Shiloh, where the two sons of Eli, Hophni and Phinehas, were priests of the LORD. On the day when Elkanah sacrificed, he would give portions to Peninnah his wife and to all her sons and daughters. But to Hannah he gave a double portion, because he loved her, though the LORD had closed her womb. And her rival used to provoke her grievously to irritate her, because the LORD had closed her womb. So it went on year by year. As often as she went up to the house of the LORD, she used to provoke her. Therefore Hannah wept and would not eat. (1 Sam. 1:1–7)

The period in which this story takes place is recorded as one of the darkest hours of Israel's history. The book of Judges ends with these telling words: "Everyone did what was right in his own eyes" (Judg. 21:25).

Not only was the nation going through a dark time, but it was also a difficult season for Hannah and her husband. Elkanah was a Levite who had two wives. Hannah, the first and favored wife, was barren and infertile. Perhaps just as Sarah decided to take care of her problem by bringing a concubine to her husband, Abraham, Elkanah may have decided to take care of his problem by adding another wife. Hannah could have even been involved in this tragic decision. The Scripture does not say how the unfortunate situation happened. It simply notes that there were two wives. Hannah, whose name means "grace," exemplified the meaning of her name. She obviously had a vital relationship and consistent walk with the Lord. The second wife was Peninnah. Peninnah had children, but Hannah had none.

Hannah's story illustrates that wherever we are, and whatever the circumstances of our lives, God never forgets or forsakes us. That does not mean we will not experience disappointment and loss—Scripture is clear that believers will suffer. Perhaps it is a mark of God's confidence when he lifts his hand from a godly woman—though for a brief time—and allows her to go through heartache and sorrow. I think of women I have known who have gone through great heartaches and trials but have maintained a steadfast trust in the Lord. I, too, want to have the kind of relationship with the Lord that will enable me to praise him, even in the dark, painful seasons of life.

We are told that Elkanah gave "portions" to Peninnah and to her sons and daughters. "But to Hannah he gave a double portion, because he loved her, though the LORD had closed her womb" (1 Sam. 1:5). Even though Hannah had not been able to produce sons or daughters, still her husband loved her devotedly. Elkanah made it a point to show that he loved Hannah, even though she had not borne the children they both desired.

Let me make a parenthetical observation here. Mothers, when you are rearing your children, remember that the man who was there before the children came will more than likely be there long after your offspring are gone. Your husband comes before your children in your spiritual priorities. Of course, part of a wife's responsibility to her husband is to care for their children, especially when the children are young. But the fact remains that your husband himself has to be your beloved as well as your lover. He is to satisfy you and be satisfied with you. Whether you have children should not affect your relationship to your husband and your responsibility to care for him. Genesis 2:24 clearly establishes God's pattern for marriage—a plan that includes leaving father and mother, clinging to one another, and becoming one flesh. There is no indication in Hannah's story that children are a prerequisite for a warm, intimate, spiritual, loving marriage. Elkanah loved Hannah, even though the Lord had closed her womb.

Twice in this passage Hannah's barrenness is attributed to the fact that "the LORD had closed her womb" (vv. 5–6). We are reminded of an easily forgotten truth—that we do not control life and death. I talk with young seminary couples who have mapped out all their plans for the next five years—including precisely when they intend to fit children into their busy lives. Yet God does not work on human timetables.

Young women have come to my office or our living room, crying because they have been trying to have a baby for six months . . . a year . . . two years. As I listen to their breaking hearts and wipe their tears, in some cases I have had to point out gently, "You have been married for a certain number of years, but your infertility has only now become a concern because bearing a child was not on your agenda until now." Though I am not debating contraception or planned childbirth, I do want to warn against giving God timetables. Every woman who has chosen to marry ought to be willing to use her God-given maternity to produce and nurture life. Women are an important part of God's plan to produce and prepare the next generation. And this awesome task must be done according to his timetable. I learned that lesson early in my own life, as I have already shared.

When my husband and I established our home, abortion was not a consideration. It was not an option. But I have to wonder now, "If I had been in the situation in which I found myself with an inconvenient pregnancy in more recent years, now that abortion is common and the 'choice' language is employed even in the religious community and the 'experts' suggest that ending an unplanned pregnancy may be the best thing for a child, what would my response have been?"

The naysayers lament that they don't want to bring children who cannot be supported properly into this cruel world. They don't want a child to be born who is not going to be able to live a "proper" life and who is not going to be "healthy." Women have been deceived into believing that they have the right to choose or deny life and to determine what quality of life is acceptable. Christian women must recognize that these decisions are not theirs to make and that issues of life and death must be surrendered to God's ultimate authority.

Hannah's plight was made even more painful by the presence of Peninnah, who would "provoke" Hannah severely and try to make her miserable because of her sealed womb. Peninnah used Hannah's infertility as a tool to heap abuse upon her rival, and she did so continually ("year by year," 1 Sam. 1:7). After a lengthy period of barrenness and taunting from Peninnah, it is not surprising that Hannah found herself in a state of despair and desperation.

Elkanah was attentive to his wife's grief and made every effort to comfort her (v. 8). But Hannah knew that the only place where she could find true comfort was in the Lord (v. 10). That assurance is one of the first marks of a woman of faith. If you aspire to be a mother committed to the Lord, if you are going to exercise the maternity that God put in your very nature in a way that pleases him, you have to know that God is the only one who can give you what you need. He alone can make you what you need to be.

Hannah knew the One who could offer help and hope to her hurting heart. As she came to the Lord in bitterness of soul, she prayed; she wept in anguish; then she made a vow—"O Lord of hosts . . . " (v. 11). When you call for the "Lord of Hosts," you can envision that a large army is on the horizon, and the Lord is at the head of this rescuing force. In Hannah's heart she must have had an understanding of the Lord as the One who does indeed lead in battle. She demonstrated deep-seated faith as she addressed the Lord in his power and might. She was saying, "I know he is able. I know he can do this."

Note the sequence of Hannah's prayer. She expressed adoration when she addressed God as "Lord of Hosts." She acknowledged his power. Then she placed her complaint before him. She cried out in effect, "I am struggling with this, Lord. I am barren. I do not understand why you have turned your back on me." Hannah recognized that only God could do something about her plight, and she made her earnest appeal to him: "Look on the affliction of your servant and remember me" (v. 11). In other words, she reminded the Lord of her own faithfulness.

At times, I have been so bold as to remind the Lord of the faithfulness of my parents and my grandparents. And when I am really agonizing with the Lord, I will say, "Lord! Here we are; we have tried to follow your will; and don't forget my mother and father and Paige's mother and father and how they faithfully walked before us. And what about our grandparents, Lord?" The Lord knows all this, but I want him to be reminded of how important the matter is to me. He wants me to come to him, realizing that he has the whole of history, including our continuing generations, in his hand.

Hannah begged the Lord not to forget her. Then she forthrightly presented her petition. She boldly asked for a male child. Why do you think she did that? Do you think it was because she did not love little girls? Or maybe she thought little girls were too fussy and hard to dress? I don't think so. Her request had been carefully fashioned in her mind and heart. She asked for a male child because she wanted to give that child back to the Lord to use in a special way. Her maternity, that nurturing instinct in her heart, responded, "Lord, this son will be my gift to you."

When I stand to give an account before the Lord Jesus Christ and have the opportunity to lay my crowns at his feet, the most valuable crowns I will have to offer will not be the conferences where I have spoken or the books I have written. The most precious gifts that I am working on for the Lord Jesus every single day of my life are my children. Let it never be that I would come to the Lord's throne without being able to lay before him the lives of Armour and Carmen and Mark and my precious granddaughters, Abigail and Rebekah. They have been the reservoir into which I have invested my energies and creativity—my life. The nurturing of my children has been an awesome task and a precious privilege.

Hannah had the same mother's heart, that same maternal longing I experienced. She said to the Lord, "Give me a son" (see v. 11). Then she presented her vow. Her prayer was not just "Give me; give me." She said to the Lord, "You give me that male child, and I will return him; I will give him to you, Lord, all the days of his life." Hannah incorporated part of the Nazirite vow in her commitment to God, promising that no razor would come upon her son's head.

There is an application suggested here, which I have used with my adult children on occasion. Hannah was bold to make commitments—even for her children. Mothers are protected in this way by Scripture. In the book of Proverbs, for example, the directives given to sons are not given to babies or children; rather, adult sons are admonished: "Forsake not your mother's teaching" (1:8). Mothers are to communicate spiritual truths to their children in order to fortify them. Even into their adult years, sons are exhorted to listen respectfully to the law of God as it is passed on from both their fathers and their mothers. So here, I believe, Hannah is claiming that role in her son's life.

When Eli the priest saw Hannah interceding so intently, he drew a wrong conclusion and spoke sharply to her. Some men look at an emotionally broken woman, and they do not understand; they may even make unkind or false accusations. What did Hannah do? Did she speak harshly to Eli or try to put him in his place? No, she answered him respectfully.

Remember the beatitude about "the poor in spirit," the humble (Matt. 5:3). Hannah had that character quality of humility. She spoke humbly to Eli (1 Sam. 1:13–16). A woman has a God-given influence and power of persuasion. She may boldly approach the throne of God. Who can persuade the Lord more effectively than a humble woman as she pours out her longings before him? God is moved when you come to him in humility, with a passion in your heart for your children and your husband.

When Eli realized the nature of Hannah's burden, he gave her some wonderful encouragement. Hannah responded simply, "Let your servant find favor in your eyes" (1 Sam. 1:18). We are reminded of Mary of Nazareth, who said, "Let it be to me according to your word" (Luke 1:38).

Now Hannah was done. She had come to the Lord, and her request had been acknowledged by God's representative. Eli had given her a good word, and her demeanor changed immediately; her face was no longer sad. Her confidence was in the Lord. She had done her part; now she went home and waited for God to fulfill his promise.

Beginning in 1 Samuel 1:19, we see the cycles in a woman's life. Hannah experienced conception; then followed the period of pregnancy. In the process of time, Hannah gave birth. She called her son Samuel, saying that she had asked the Lord for him. Hannah knew in her heart that she had asked, and the Lord had heard and responded.

The picture of Hannah nursing her son at her breast (v. 23) depicts the tremendous capacity for love that is in a mother's heart. God uses the relationship of a nursing mother with her child to describe the depth of his love and compassion, and he likens this relationship to his relationship with his people (Isa. 49:15).

Mothers have the first opportunity to introduce God to their infants. Before an infant can ever understand words or read the Bible or memorize Bible verses, he learns about God and how the Lord cares for him by means of a mother's touch and through a mother's love, nourishment, and comfort. The mothers of both Samuel and Moses only had their children during those early, nursing years. Yet in that brief time they were able to give their sons all they needed in order to stand firm for the Lord and to become great leaders for him.

The Lord granted Hannah's petition, and she kept her vow to him. As soon as her son was weaned, she delivered him to the house of the Lord in Shiloh. Samuel served the Lord and his nation faithfully; he made his mother proud. Though Hannah had her son in the family circle for only a few years, she made a mark on his life; she nurtured him physically and spiritually. Her efforts were rewarded by a son who was faithful to the Lord (1 Sam. 2:26; 3:19–20). God grant that we, like Hannah, may gladly fulfill our holy calling to be givers and nurturers of life and that we may give back to his service those whom he has entrusted to our care.

OLDER WOMEN
MENTORING YOUNGER WOMEN:
TITUS 2
IN THE CHURCH TODAY

Susan Hunt

As for you, teach what accords with sound doctrine. . . . Older women likewise are to be reverent in behavior, not slanderers or slaves to much wine. They are to teach what is good, and so train the young women to love their husbands and children, to be self-controlled, pure, working at home, kind, and submissive to their own husbands, that the word of God may not be reviled.

TITUS 2:1, 3-5

THIS MANDATE IS ELECTRIFYING! Titus was pastoring a church on the island of Crete. The prevailing culture was pluralistic and decadent. Of all the things Paul could have told Titus to tell the women to do to combat that decadence, he bore down on the importance of older women encouraging and equipping younger women to live godly lives.

This was not a new concept. Throughout the Old Testament we are told that one generation is to tell the next generation the praiseworthy deeds of the Lord. In Titus 2, that characteristic of covenant life is simply made gender-specific. This fundamental quality of the culture of covenant life transcends time, geography, life-season, and life-circumstance.

Everywhere I go I meet young women who long for spiritual mothers. Some express a sense of loneliness, and yet they do not even realize that the disconnection they feel is because they do not have nurturing relationships with older women. Our postmodern age is characterized by isolation. The feminist movement made many promises, but the push for independence and autonomy has left women confused and alone. This is our opportunity. The time is ripe. Women are seeking answers. It is time for Christian women to step into this vacuum and show and tell the truth about womanhood.

But where are the older women?

In recent years I have observed a troubling phenomenon. Many women of my generation have relinquished this high calling of nurturing younger women. My generation has abandoned this calling for many reasons. Some simply do not know this biblical mandate. The church has not sounded this call for many decades. Some think they have nothing to offer. Some are intimidated by the intelligence and giftedness of younger women. Some have decided this is the season to indulge themselves. Some want to share their life experiences, but they feel isolated from the younger women and don't know how to bridge that gap.

I plead with the church to call and equip women for this ministry. God is gifting his church with incredible young women. They are a sacred trust. We must be good stewards of this gift. Many are first-generation Christians. Many are separated from their extended families because of the mobility of our society. We must exemplify the faith to them, and we must teach them how to show and tell the truths of biblical womanhood to the next generation. The implications of whether we accept or abandon this calling will reverberate for generations to come.

As we examine Paul's mandate to Titus, your mind may be buzzing with questions: am I an older woman or a younger woman? What do spiritual mothering relationships look like? How do I find them? Why should I make this kind of investment in the life of a younger woman?

We'll address those questions, but first we must step back and see the landscape on which spiritual mothering relationships are to be crafted and lived out.

THE COVENANT OF GRACE

God relates to us on the basis of a covenant of grace.

> "For you are a people holy to the LORD your God. The LORD your God has chosen you to be a people for his treasured possession, out of all the peoples who are on the face of the earth. It was not because you were more in number than any other people that the LORD set his love on you and chose you, for you were the fewest of all peoples, but it is because the LORD loves you and is keeping the oath that he swore to your fathers, that the LORD has brought you out with a mighty hand and redeemed you from the house of slavery, from the hand of Pharaoh king of Egypt. Know therefore that the LORD your God is God, the faithful God who keeps covenant and steadfast love with those who love him and keep his commandments, to a thousand generations." (Deut. 7:6–9)

Our relationship with the Lord is personal, but it is not individualistic. When he adopts us into his family, our relationship with him means that we are also related to his other children. And our relationships with one another are to mirror our Father's relationship with us.

> May the God of endurance and encouragement grant you to live in such harmony with one another, in accord with Christ Jesus, that together you may with one voice glorify the God and Father of our Lord Jesus Christ. Therefore welcome one another as Christ has welcomed you, for the glory of God. (Rom. 15:5–7)

How does Christ accept us? Not on the basis of our performance, but on the basis of his grace. We do not earn our relationship with the Lord. It is all through sovereign grace from eternity past, when he set his affection upon us, to the moment in history when he gives us a new heart so we can repent and believe, to eternity future. God forgives us because Jesus paid our penalty, and he accepts us into his presence because we are covered with the righteousness of Christ. This is the covenant of grace.

We are to accept, love, and care for one another on the same term by which God accepts us—grace. The covenant way is not a way of isolation and independence.

When Cain killed his brother Abel, the Lord asked him "'Where is Abel your brother?' He said, 'I do not know; am I my brother's keeper?'" (Gen. 4:9). He was unaware that the answer to that question is yes. Living covenantally means that we are our brother's and sister's keeper. Women nurturing women is simply one way we live covenantally. It is as much a part of covenant life as gathering at the Lord's Table to remember Jesus' death until he comes again.

It is not optional. This gospel imperative is one way we express our Lord's command to love him with all our heart, soul, and mind and to love our neighbor as we love ourselves (Matt. 22:37–39).

UNPACKING THE PASSAGE

Now let's take a closer look at Titus 2.

To whom is this mandate given? It is interesting to note that this mandate is not written to women. It is written to the pastor of a church. It is a responsibility of church leadership to equip older women for this ministry. Women nurturing women is an essential element of healthy church life.

What is the foundation for this mandate? Titus 2 relationships are not to happen in a vacuum. They are to take place within the context of sound doctrine.

> Paul's instruction to Titus to teach the women morality based on sound doctrine implies that the women were to be taught doctrine. . . . So these women were to be taught the principles of the Christian faith which would form the basis for their character. The soundness, or correctness, of the doctrine would give them a foundation from which to train the younger women.
>
> Sound doctrine qualifies the kind of morality Paul is advocating in the command. Morality must be based on who God is and what He has done for us in Christ, or it will be purely subjective. Unless God is the reference point, there is no objective, absolute standard or authority for morality. If we begin anywhere else, our morality will degenerate to the level of the moral code of our environment. . . .
>
> Apparently Paul did not expect or want the women in the Cretan church to change their conduct without changing their thinking. He wanted them to think Christianly so that they would act Christianly. And sound doctrine is essential for right thinking.[1]

What is the purpose of this mandate? The emphasis of the book of Titus is sound doctrine and godly living. God's glory is the over-riding purpose of the relationships being discussed. This is not a self-enrichment program. These are covenant relationships that are centered on glorifying God by reflecting his grace to one another. In *Spiritual Mothering*, I give the following definition:

> **Spiritual Mothering:** When a woman possessing faith and spiritual maturity enters into a nurturing relationship with a younger woman in order to encourage and equip her to live for God's glory.[2]

What kind of training is involved? The word translated "train" (Titus 2:4) is the Greek word *sophronizo*. It denotes "to cause to be of sound mind, to recall to one's senses. . . . The training would involve the cultivation of sound judgment and prudence. It suggests the exercise of that self-restraint that governs all passions and desires, enabling the believer to be conformed to the mind of Christ."[3] This is not just formal Bible instruction. This is teaching a way of life as we live in relationship with one another. It is passing on to younger women a biblical worldview that includes a biblical perspective of womanhood. It is helping them to think biblically and to apply biblical truth to all of life.

Who are the older women? This is not just about chronological age. It also involves life experiences and spiritual maturity. Every woman is both a younger and an older woman. There is someone who needs your life-perspective, and there is someone with a life-view that you need.

HOW DOES A WOMEN'S MINISTRY IMPLEMENT A TITUS 2 MINISTRY?

How do older and younger women find each other? The easiest way is when a church crafts a substantive women's ministry that teaches women God's truth about womanhood and helps facilitate covenant relationships that reflect our relationship with God.

The Titus 2 mandate is not a program—it is a lifestyle. However, it often takes some programming to jump-start spiritual mothering relationships. Here are a few suggestions to help a women's ministry leadership team encourage and equip women for a Titus 2 ministry.

GENERAL OBSERVATIONS

First, the women's leadership team needs to have a deep and long-term commitment to this scriptural mandate. It is not simply a matter of matching older women and younger women. This is a part of covenant life. Paul says that it is essential "that the word of God may not be reviled" (Titus 2:5).

Second, it is important for the leadership team to have their finger on the pulse of the women. Is spiritual mothering happening spontaneously and informally? If so, there may not be a need for a formal program. Perhaps the need is to simply celebrate what is happening by periodically asking women to share testimonies of how other women in the covenant community nurture them in the faith. Or if there are women who are on the fringe of church life or new believers who did not grow up in Christian homes, perhaps a spiritual mothering program is a way to enfold and nurture them.

Third, the Titus mandate was given to the pastor of the church. Paul instructed young Titus to equip older women in the congregation for this ministry. This equipping was to take place within the context of sound doctrine. It is a part of healthy church life. It is not just a *women's thing*. The commitment of church leadership is biblical and essential. If a decision is made to have a formal program, it is important to have the oversight and protection of the elders.

Consider this possible scenario: you announce that you are beginning a Titus 2 program, and you ask for volunteers to be spiritual mothers. A woman who has recently joined the church and appears to have great experience and maturity enthusiastically volunteers. You are unaware that she holds some theological positions and some views about women and marriage that are not consistent with Scripture. She is assigned to a young woman who, unknown to you, is having difficulties in her marriage because she resists the idea of headship and submission. Since such women who volunteer to be spiritual mothers have received no training, guidelines, accountability structure, or approved list of books to study, you have a disaster waiting to happen.

Fourth, careful and prayerful thought should be given to potential implications of a spiritual mothering program.

- How will spiritual mothers be selected?
- What accountability will spiritual mothers have and to whom?
- How can you avoid having young women disappointed because their spiritual mothers never cultivate the relationship?
- Who will monitor the program to see that it maintains its purpose and integrity?
- How will this program interface with the entire Christian education program of the church?

Fifth, even if it is decided to have a formal spiritual mothering program, women should be taught that this is to be a way of life and that the Lord will guide many women into nurturing relationships without the aid of a program. The legitimacy of these informal relationships should be highlighted and celebrated. The more a covenant community understands that this is part and parcel of community life, the less need there is for a formal program.

Sixth, spiritual mothering is not just a matter of chronological age. Even if all of the women in the church are the same age, there will be various levels of spiritual maturity and life experiences that equip them to nurture one another.

Seventh, the Titus 2 mandate is not limited to married women. Women should have a generational vision that includes singles, teens, and even little girls. Covenant daughters should be taught biblical womanhood by the women in the covenant community.

Eighth, if the elders and the women's leadership team determine that there is a need for a formal Titus 2 ministry, a subcommittee could be appointed to develop the purpose, procedures, policies, and plans. Simultaneously, enlist a prayer team to pray regularly for this committee. All plans should be submitted to the women's leadership team and then to the elders for approval. Elders may need to consider establishing policies for situations that will be referred to them.

SUGGESTIONS FOR A TITUS 2 MINISTRY PLANNING SUBCOMMITTEE

1) Determine the Purpose of the Titus 2 Ministry

For example: "The purpose of the women's ministry Titus 2 program is to help women establish covenant relationships with godly, older women who will encourage and equip them to live for God's glory."

2) Develop a Plan to Enlist and Train Spiritual Mothers

This plan should clearly state the qualifications, how women will be recruited, how they will be approved by the elders, and how they will be accountable to the women's leadership team.

The training should be consistent with the doctrines and vision of the church. A "curriculum" should also include overarching principles of biblical womanhood. (*Biblical Foundations for Womanhood* is a series of books that are designed to train women to have a biblical perspective of womanhood and thus to equip them for a Titus 2 ministry.[4])

In some cases, a women's ministry may offer these studies through a Bible study program and then, growing out of that, identify women who are ready to be spiritual mothers. This long-term approach means that it will take several months for the training phase before moving to the next level of actually beginning the Titus 2 ministry.

Another option is to identify the spiritual mothers and then take them through the studies in a condensed format. They can read a book on their own, come together to discuss it, and then move to the next book. This could even be done in a training retreat.

This training should include a plan to train and enlist additional spiritual mothers in the future. Spiritual mothers should be trained to reproduce by encouraging their spiritual daughters to have the goal of becoming spiritual mothers themselves.

3) Determine the Target Audience

The number of spiritual mothers will determine the scope of the program. It is likely that the number of women desiring spiritual mothers will exceed the number of spiritual mothers. The purpose of the program should help determine which women will have priority in being assigned spiritual mothers. For example, you may target women who are not able to attend regular women's ministry Bible studies and encourage those who do attend these studies to engage them in informal Titus 2 relationships.

When there are enough trained spiritual mothers, you may want to consider expanding the program to enfold teenage girls. Another long-term objective could be to provide a spiritual mother for every new female member of the church for three months.

4) Develop Guidelines

Develop guidelines that include things such as:

- How spiritual mothers and daughters will be matched. This can be as simple as drawing names or as involved as finding common interests and experiences. Whatever method is used, the most important thing is to spend much time praying for the Lord to bring the women together according to His purposes for them.
- The duration of the formal relationship. Usually it is recommended that a spiritual mothering program run a year at a time.
- How to determine the shape of the relationship. Spiritual mothers should be encouraged to have good conversations with their spiritual daughters to ascertain needs, expectations, and realistic goals. Will they meet at a regular time or will it be more informal? Will they study and pray together or just meet for lunch and conversation?
- A list of approved books for spiritual mothers and daughters to read and discuss.
- How and where to refer problems that require pastoral or professional help. This should include cautions and clear parameters about dealing with crisis situations.
- How the program will be publicized. Publicity should be a tool to educate the entire congregation about the purpose of the program and to enlist prayer support.

5) Outline a Plan

Outline a plan to maintain the vision and heart of the program. For example:

- Have two or three gatherings a year for those involved in the program. This could include a sharing time, so the participants can learn from and encourage one another.
- Each year before women sign up for the program, promote it by having spiritual mothers/daughters give brief testimonies in church. Have a different testimony for each of three or four Sundays before the sign-up begins.
- At women's ministry special events, have women share testimonies about the blessings of Titus 2 relationships.

6) Develop a Plan

Develop a plan to implement the program. For example:

- There should be a Titus 2 coordinator or committee. Determine how this person/committee will be appointed, length of term, and how she or they will relate to the women's ministry leadership team.
- Women who complete the course of study will be asked to pray about becoming spiritual mothers. Those who are willing will fill out a form agreeing to the guidelines. These names will be submitted to the elders for approval. Those approved will be commissioned in a church service. They will commit to pray throughout the summer for the Lord to direct the committee in assigning them a spiritual daughter.
- The committee will determine how many spiritual daughters the program can accommodate, offer the program to the women, make assignments, and host a gathering for the spiritual mothers and daughters.
- At the end of the term, the committee will meet with spiritual mothers for evaluation, ask if they will serve again, and get their recommendations of spiritual daughters who completed all the studies and who may be ready to be spiritual mothers. In some instances a spiritual mother and daughter may want to continue for another year in order to complete the entire course of study. The committee will also determine if they need to provide another training time for women who may be interested in becoming spiritual mothers.
- Every opportunity will be used to keep the Titus 2 concept before the women at large through testimonies at special events, articles in newsletters, and public prayer for spiritual mothers.

THE GOAL

The goal of a Titus 2 ministry is not a dazzling, well-run ministry. Paul told the young preacher to equip older women with sound doctrine so they could train younger women "that the word of God may not be reviled" (v. 5). This is compelling. It is a gospel imperative. It is the way Christian women show and tell the next generation of women "the glorious deeds of the LORD, and his might, and the wonders that he has done . . . that the next generation might know them, the children yet unborn, and arise and tell them to their children, so that they should set their hope in God and not forget the works of God, but keep his commandments" (Ps. 78:4, 6–7).

And thus Christendom is advanced.

CONCLUSION

WE INVITE YOU TO TAKE TIME TO reflect on some of the Scriptures we have considered.

The wisest of women builds her house,
but folly with her own hands tears it down. (Prov. 14:1)

I praise you, for I am fearfully and wonderfully made.
Wonderful are your works;
my soul knows it very well." (Ps. 139:14)

"It is not good that the man should be alone; I will make him a helper fit for him." (Gen. 2:18)

Charm is deceitful, and beauty is vain. (Prov. 31:30)

Do not let your adorning be external—the braiding of hair and the putting on of gold jewelry, or the clothing you wear—but let your adorning be the hidden person of the heart with the imperishable beauty of a gentle and quiet spirit, which in God's sight is very precious. For this is how the holy women who hoped in God used to adorn themselves. (1 Pet. 3:3–5)

Older women likewise are to be reverent in behavior, not slanderers or slaves to much wine. They are to teach what is good, and so train the young women to love their husbands and children, to be self-controlled, pure, working at home, kind, and submissive to their own husbands, that the word of God may not be reviled. (Titus 2:3–5)

Women should adorn themselves in respectable apparel, with modesty and self-control, not with braided hair and gold or pearls or costly attire, but with what is proper for women who profess godliness—with good works. (1 Tim. 2:9–10)

As God said, "I will make my dwelling among them and walk among them, and I will be their God, and they shall be my people. . . . And I will be a father to you, and you shall be sons and daughters to me, says the Lord Almighty." (2 Cor. 6:16, 18)

And because you are sons, God has sent the Spirit of his Son into our hearts, crying, "Abba! Father!" (Gal. 4:6)

Who shall separate us from the love of Christ? Shall tribulation, or distress, or persecution, or famine, or nakedness, or danger, or sword? As it is written,

"For your sake we are being killed all the day long;
    we are regarded as sheep to be slaughtered."

    No, in all these things we are more than conquerors through him who loved us. For I am sure that neither death nor life, nor angels nor rulers, nor things present nor things to come, nor powers, nor height nor depth, nor anything else in all creation, will be able to separate us from the love of God in Christ Jesus our Lord. (Rom. 8:35–39)

"I am the true vine, and my Father is the vinedresser. Every branch in me that does not bear fruit he takes away, and every branch that does bear fruit he prunes, that it may bear more fruit." (John 15:1–2)

"I will give them a heart to know that I am the LORD, and they shall be my people and I will be their God, for they shall return to me with their whole heart." (Jer. 24:7)

An excellent wife who can find?
    She is far more precious than jewels.
The heart of her husband trusts in her,
    and he will have no lack of gain.
She does him good, and not harm,
    all the days of her life. . . .
She opens her mouth with wisdom,
    and the teaching of kindness is on her tongue.
She looks well to the ways of her household
    and does not eat the bread of idleness.
Her children rise up and call her blessed;
    her husband also, and he praises her:
"Many women have done excellently,

but you surpass them all."
Charm is deceitful, and beauty is vain,
　　but a woman who fears the LORD is to be praised.
Give her of the fruit of her hands,
　　and let her works praise her in the gates.
　　(Prov. 31:10–12, 26–31)

RECOMMENDED RESOURCES

THE FOLLOWING RESOURCES will give further insight, stimulate your thinking, and encourage your heart as you seek to become God's true woman.

To the best of our knowledge, we believe these resources are faithful to the Scripture. However, inclusion in this list does not necessarily imply our unqualified endorsement of the authors, resources, or organizations represented. God expects every believer to examine all input in the light of his Word.

BIBLICAL WOMANHOOD

Council on Biblical Manhood and Womanhood. *The Danvers Statement: 20th Anniversary Edition.* Louisville: Council on Biblical Manhood and Womanhood, 2007; http://www.cbmw.org/Danvers.

DeMoss, Nancy Leigh. *Biblical Portrait of Womanhood: Discovering and Living Out God's Plan for Our Lives.* © 2008, Revive Our Hearts.

Grudem, Wayne, ed. *Biblical Foundations for Manhood and Womanhood.* Wheaton, IL: Crossway Books, 2002.

———. *Countering the Claims of Evangelical Feminism: Biblical Responses to the Key Questions.* Sisters, OR: Multnomah, 2006.

———. *Evangelical Feminism: A New Path to Liberalism?* Wheaton, IL: Crossway Books, 2006.

———. *Evangelical Feminism and Biblical Truth: An Analysis of More Than 100 Disputed Questions.* Sisters, OR: Multnomah, 2004.

Hunt, Susan. *By Design: God's Distinctive Calling for Women.* Wheaton, IL: Crossway Books, 1998.

Hunt, Susan, and Barbara Thompson. *The Legacy of Biblical Womanhood.* Wheaton, IL: Crossway Books, 2003.

Impson, Beth. *Called to Womanhood: The Biblical View for Today's World.* Wheaton, IL: Crossway Books, 2001.

Jones, Rebecca. *Does Christianity Squash Women? A Christian Looks at Womanhood*. Nashville: Broadman and Holman, 2005.

Kassian, Mary. *The Feminist Mistake: The Radical Impact of Feminism on Church and Culture*. Wheaton, IL: Crossway Books, 2005.

———. *Women, Creation, and the Fall*. Wheaton, IL: Crossway Books, 1990.

Köstenberger, Andreas J., Thomas R. Schreiner, and H. Scott Baldwin, eds. *Women in the Church: A Fresh Analysis of 1 Timothy 2:9–15*. Grand Rapids, MI: Baker, 2005.

MacArthur, John. *Twelve Extraordinary Women: How God Shaped Women of the Bible, and What He Wants to Do with You*. Nashville: Thomas Nelson, 2005.

McCulley, Carolyn. *Radical Womanhood: Feminine Faith in a Feminist World*. Chicago: Moody, forthcoming 2008.

Piper, John. *What's the Difference? Manhood and Womanhood Defined According to the Bible*. Wheaton, IL: Crossway Books, 2001.

Piper, John and Wayne Grudem. *50 Crucial Questions: An Overview of Central Concerns About Manhood and Womanhood*. Louisville: Council on Biblical Manhood and Womanhood, 1992.

———, eds. *Recovering Biblical Manhood and Womanhood: A Response to Evangelical Feminism*. Wheaton, IL: Crossway Books, 2006.

Strauch, Alexander. *Men and Women, Equal Yet Different: A Brief Study of the Biblical Passages on Gender*. Colorado Springs: Lewis and Roth, 1999.

Wilson, Nancy. *The Fruit of Her Hands: Respect and the Christian Woman*. Moscow, ID: Canon Press, 1997.

Wilson, P. B. *Liberated Through Submission: God's Design for Freedom in All Relationships*. Eugene, OR: Harvest, 2007.

MARRIAGE AND FAMILY

Carder, Dave. *Torn Asunder: Recovering from Extramarital Affairs*. Chicago: Moody, 2001.

Cobb, Nancy, and Connie Grigsby. *The Politically Incorrect Wife: God's Plan for Marriage Still Works Today*. Sisters, OR: Multnomah, 2003.

DeMoss, Nancy Leigh. *Singled Out for Him: Embracing the Gift, the Blessings, and the Challenges of Singleness*. Niles, MI: Revive Our Hearts, 1998.

Dillow, Linda, and Lorraine Pintus. *Intimate Issues: 21 Questions Christian Women Ask About Sex*. Colorado Springs: Waterbrook, 1999.

Easley, Cindy. *What's Submission Got to Do with It? Find Out From a Woman Like You*. Chicago: Moody, 2008.

Ennis, Pat, and Lisa Tatlock. *Practicing Hospitality: The Joy of Serving Others*. Wheaton, IL: Crossway Books, 2008.

Eggerichs, Emerson. *Love and Respect: The Love She Most Desires; The Respect He Desperately Needs*. Nashville: Thomas Nelson, 2004.

Feldhahn, Shaunti. *For Women Only: What You Need to Know About the Inner Lives of Men*. Sisters, OR: Multnomah, 2004.

Fitzpatrick, Elyse. *Helper by Design: God's Perfect Plan for Women in Marriage*. Chicago: Moody, 2003.

Harvey, Dave. *When Sinners Say "I Do": Discovering the Power of the Gospel for Marriage*. Wapwallopen, PA: Shepherd Press, 2007.

Hunt, Susan. *Your Home: A Place of Grace*. Wheaton, IL: Crossway Books, 2000.

Kennedy, Nancy. *When He Doesn't Believe: Help and Encouragement for Women Who Feel Alone in Their Faith*. Colorado Springs: WaterBrook, 2001.

Köstenberger, Andreas. *God, Marriage, and Family: Rebuilding the Biblical Foundation*. Wheaton, IL: Crossway Books, 2004.

Mahaney, Carolyn. *Feminine Appeal: Seven Virtues of a Godly Wife and Mother*. Wheaton, IL: Crossway Books, 2004.

McCulley, Carolyn. *Did I Kiss Marriage Goodbye? Trusting God with a Hope Deferred*. Wheaton, IL: Crossway Books, 2004.

Omartian, Stormie. *The Power of a Praying Wife*. Eugene, OR: Harvest, 1997.

Peace, Martha. *The Excellent Wife: A Biblical Perspective*. Bemidji, MN: Focus, 1999.

Peace, Martha, and John Crotts. *Tying the Knot Tighter: Because Marriage Lasts a Lifetime*. Phillipsburg, NJ: P&R, 2007.

Piper, John. *Stewards of a Great Mystery*. Louisville: Council on Biblical Manhood and Womanhood.

Plowman, Ginger. *Heaven at Home: Establishing and Enjoying a Peaceful Home*. Wapwallopen, PA: Shepherd Press, 2006.

Rainey, Dennis, ed. *Building Strong Families*. Wheaton, IL: Crossway Books, 2002.

Rainey, Dennis, and Barbara Rainey. *Moments Together for Intimacy: Devotions for Drawing Near to God and One Another.* Little Rock: Family Life Publishing, 2003.

Titus, Devi, and Marilyn Weiher. *The Home Experience: Making Your Home a Sanctuary of Love and a Haven of Peace.* Living Smart Resources, 2007. http://www.mentoringmansion.com/

PARENTING

Clarkson, Sally. *The Ministry of Motherhood: Following Christ's Example in Reaching the Hearts of Our Children.* Colorado Springs: Waterbrook, 2004.

———. *The Mission of Motherhood: Touching Your Child's Heart for Eternity.* Colorado Springs: Waterbrook, 2003.

Courtney, Vicki. *Your Boy: Raising a Godly Son in an Ungodly World.* Nashville: Broadman and Holman, 2006.

———. *Your Girl: Raising a Godly Daughter in an Ungodly World.* Nashville: Broadman and Holman, 2004.

DeMoss, Nancy Leigh and Dannah Gresh. *Lies Young Women Believe: And the Truth That Sets Them Free.* Chicago: Moody, 2008.

Elliot, Elisabeth. *The Shaping of a Christian Family.* York: Revell, 2000.

Farris, Vickie, and Jayme Farris Metzgar. *A Mom Just Like You.* Broadman and Holman, 2002.

Fitzpatrick, Elyse, and Jim Newheiser. *When Good Kids Make Bad Choices.* Eugene, OR: Harvest, 2005.

Fleming, Jean. *A Mother's Heart: A Look at Values, Vision, and Character for the Christian Mother.* Colorado Springs: NavPress, 1996.

Hunt, Susan. *Heirs of the Covenant: Leaving a Legacy for the Next Generation.* Wheaton, IL: Crossway Books, 1998.

Hunter, Brenda. *Home by Choice: Raising Emotionally Secure Children in an Insecure World.* Sisters, OR: Multnomah, 2000.

Jaynes, Sharon. *Being a Great Mom, Raising Great Kids.* Chicago: Moody, 2004.

Mahaney, Carolyn, and Nicole Mahaney Whitacre. *Girl Talk: Mother-Daughter Conversations on Biblical Womanhood.* Wheaton, IL: Crossway Books, 2005.

Miller, Donna J., and Christine Yount. *Growing Little Women: Capturing Teachable Moments with Your Daughter.* Chicago: Moody, 1997.

——. *Growing Little Women for Younger Girls: Capturing Teachable Moments with Your Daughter*. Chicago: Moody, 2000.

Nichols, Fern, and Janet Kobobel Grant. *Every Child Needs a Praying Mom*. Grand Rapids: Zondervan, 2003.

Omartian, Stormie. *The Power of a Praying Parent*. Eugene, OR: Harvest, 1995.

Otto, Donna. *Finding Your Purpose as a Mom: How to Build Your Home on Holy Ground*. Eugene, OR: Harvest: 2004.

Patterson, Dorothy Kelley. *Where's Mom? The High Calling of Wives and Mothers*. Wheaton, IL: Crossway Books, 2003.

Plowman, Ginger. *Don't Make Me Count to Three: A Mom's Look at Heart-Oriented Discipline*. Wapwallopen, PA: Shepherd Press, 2004.

Rainey, Barbara, and Susan Yates. *Barbara and Susan's Guide to the Empty Nest: Discovering New Purpose, Passion and Your Next Great Adventure*. Little Rock: Family Life Publishing, 2008.

Rainey, Dennis, and Barbara Rainey, and Bruce Nygren. *Parenting Today's Adolescent: Helping Your Child Avoid the Traps of the Preteen and Teen Years*. Nashville: Thomas Nelson, 2002.

Tripp, Paul David. *Age of Opportunity: A Biblical Guide to Parenting Teens*. Phillipsburg, NJ: P&R, 2001.

Tripp, Tedd. *Shepherding a Child's Heart*. Wapwallopen, PA: Shepherd Press, 1998.

Tripp, Tedd, and Margy Tripp. *Instructing a Child's Heart*. Wapwallopen, PA: Shepherd Press, 2008.

PURITY

Alcorn, Randy. *The Purity Principle: God's Safeguards for Life's Dangerous Trails*. Sisters, OR: Multnomah, 2003.

Anderson, Nancy C. *Avoiding the Greener Grass Syndrome: How to Grow Affair Proof Hedges Around Your Marriage*. Grand Rapids: Kregel, 2004.

Bishop, Jennie. *The Princess and the Kiss: A Story of God's Gift of Purity*. Anderson, IN: Warner Press, 2000.

——. *The Squire and the Scroll*. Anderson, IN: Warner Press, 2004

Bishop, Jennie, and Susan Henson. *Life Lessons from the Princess and the Kiss*. Niles, MI: Revive Our Hearts, 2004

——. *Life Lessons from the Squire and the Scroll*. Niles, MI: Revive Our Hearts, 2005.

DeMoss, Nancy Leigh. *Modesty: Does God Really Care What I Wear?* Buchanan, MI: Revive Our Hearts, 2003.

Elliot, Elisabeth. *Passion and Purity: Learning to Bring Your Love Life Under Christ's Control.* Grand Rapids: Revell, 2002.

Gresh, Dannah. *And the Bride Wore White: Seven Secrets to Sexual Purity.* Chicago: Moody, 2004.

Hall, Laurie. *An Affair of the Mind.* Colorado Springs: Focus on the Family, 1998.

Harris, Joshua. *Sex is Not the Problem (Lust Is): Sexual Purity in a Lust-Saturated World.* Sisters, OR: Multnomah, 2005.

Jenkins, Jerry. *Hedges: Loving Your Marriage Enough to Protect It.* Wheaton, IL: Crossway Books, 2005.

Piper, John, and Justin Taylor, eds. *Sex and the Supremacy of Christ.* Wheaton, IL: Crossway Books, 2005.

Starr, Judy. *The Enticement of the Forbidden.* Life Connexions, 2004.

SPIRITUAL GROWTH

DeMoss, Nancy Leigh. *Lies Women Believe: And the Truth That Sets Them Free.* Chicago: Moody, 2002.

———. *A Place of Quiet Rest: Finding Intimacy with God Through a Daily Devotional Life.* Chicago: Moody, 2002.

Elliot, Elisabeth. *Let Me Be a Woman.* Wheaton, IL: Tyndale, 1999.

Ennis, Pat. *Precious in His Sight: The Fine Art of Becoming a Godly Woman.* Sisters, OR: Trusted Books, 2006.

Ennis, Pat, and Lisa Tatlock. *Becoming a Woman Who Pleases God: A Guide to Developing Your Biblical Potential.* Chicago: Moody, 2003.

George, Elizabeth. *Beautiful in God's Eyes: The Treasures of the Proverbs 31 Woman.* Sisters, OR: Harvest, 2005.

———. *Loving God with All Your Mind.* Eugene, OR: Harvest, 2005.

———. *A Woman After God's Own Heart.* Sisters, OR: Harvest, 2006.

Hughes, Barbara. *Disciplines of a Godly Woman.* Wheaton, IL: Crossway Books, 2006.

Hunt, Susan. *The True Woman: The Beauty and Strength of a Godly Woman.* Wheaton, IL: Crossway Books, 1997.

Jaynes, Sharon. *The Power of a Woman's Words.* Eugene, OR: Harvest, 2007.

Kassian, Mary. *In My Father's House: Finding Your Heart's True Home.* Nashville: Broadman and Holman, 2005.

Ortlund, Anne. *The Gentle Ways of a Beautiful Woman: A Practical Guide to Spiritual Beauty.* Nashville: Thomas Nelson, 2004.

Ortlund, Jani. *Fearlessly Feminine: Boldly Living God's Plan for Womanhood.* Sisters, OR: Multnomah, 2000.

Patterson, Dorothy Kelley. *A Woman Seeking God: Discover God in the Places of Your Life.* Nashville: Broadman and Holman, 1992.

Peace, Martha. *Damsels in Distress: Biblical Solutions for Problems Women Face.* Phillipsburg, NJ: P&R, 2006.

WOMEN'S MINISTRY

Duncan, J. Ligon and Susan Hunt. *Women's Ministry in the Local Church.* Wheaton, IL: Crossway Books, 2006.

Fitzpatrick, Elyse, and Carol Cornish. *Women Helping Women: A Biblical Guide to Major Issues Women Face.* Eugene, OR: Harvest, 1997.

Hunt, Susan. *Spiritual Mothering: The Titus 2 Model for Women Mentoring Women.* Wheaton, IL: Crossway Books, 1993.

Hunt, Susan, and Peggy Hutcheson. *Leadership for Women in the Church.* Grand Rapids: Zondervan, 1991.

THINKING IT OVER
AND MAKING IT PERSONAL

THIS SECTION IS INTENDED TO stimulate further thought and interaction with the themes of this book. The questions below can be used for personal reflection or (ideally) for discussion with one or more friends who share your desire to become "God's true woman."

If you are using this guide as part of a group study, you may wish to cover one or more chapters each time you meet, depending on the format and length of your study. The objective is not to get through all the questions but to dialogue in a meaningful way about the content of each chapter and to provide opportunity for the Holy Spirit to search your heart and to show you how to apply what you have read to your current life season and circumstances.

If you are meeting with others, consider including these components in each session:

- Open in prayer, asking God to give you understanding of his ways and to give you a heart to receive and respond to his Truth.
- Share any insights from the chapter(s) you read that you found particularly helpful, encouraging, or challenging.
- Discuss some or all of the suggested questions.
- Share any areas of your life where God has shown you a need for change or growth, based on your reading and discussion.
- Pray for each other as you seek to live out God's calling in your lives. Humbly acknowledge your need for his grace and the power of his Spirit to fulfill that calling. Pray about specific issues or areas of need that those in the group may be facing.

INTRODUCTION

1) How would you summarize the "revolution" highlighted in *Time* magazine's special 1990 issue on women?

2) What were some of the "promises" of that revolution? How would you assess the outcome and impact of the feminist revolution? To what extent do you think its promises have been fulfilled?

3) What negative consequences of that revolution can be seen today in women's lives, in the home, in our culture, and in the church?

4) In what ways have many Christian women's lives—their thinking, values, priorities, choices—been influenced by the world's view of what it means to be a successful woman? Can you identify any ways that you have been influenced by the world's perspective on womanhood?

5) In your own words, describe the "counterrevolution" Nancy calls us to believe God for. What might such a movement among Christian women look like? What might help bring about such a movement in our day?

6) Discuss the prayer by John Greenleaf Whittier on p. 19. What petitions does he make? How does this prayer express a dependence on the character and grace of God to fulfill his purposes in our lives?

7) Take time to personalize Whittier's prayer for your life and for the others in your group. Ask God to use you to create hunger and thirst in other Christian women for a spiritual "counterrevolution."

CHAPTER 1: FEMININITY

1) Name one or more women you admired as a young girl. What drew you to them?

2) If a young teen asked you to explain the difference between "feminine" and "masculine," what would you say?

3) What models does society offer for femininity? How does society define womanly success?

4) Carolyn quotes Susan Brownmiller as saying, "Women are all female impersonators to some degree" and "femininity, in essence, is a romantic sentiment, a nostalgic tradition of imposed limitations." How would you respond to these ideas? Use Scripture if you can.

5) What are some of the biblical arguments for the belief that femininity is not culturally imposed?

6) Read Genesis 1:27. What are some of the implications of the fact that "God created man in his own image . . . male and female he created them"?

7) Discuss John Piper's definition of "mature femininity" (p. 25). What are some practical ways this kind of femininity might be expressed in the life of a married woman? A single woman?

8) How are "life-bearing," "nurturing," and "love of home" related to a biblical view of femininity? How can single women or married women without children fulfill these aspects of true womanhood?

9) Share some examples of how you have seen women exemplify true femininity. How can Christian women glorify God in our world through their femininity?

10) What areas did God lay on your heart as you read this chapter? Are there specific ways you could express godly femininity to a greater extent?

CHAPTER 2: TRUE BEAUTY

1) What is something you have done to change your appearance that in retrospect seems ridiculous or excessive (think makeup, clothing, or hair styles, fad diets, restricting body shapers, body piercings, plastic surgery, etc.)?

2) What influences contribute to contemporary women being so obsessed with their appearance? What underlying sins are involved in this preoccupation?

3) In Scripture, do you think outward beauty is portrayed as more of a blessing or a curse? What dangers come with outward beauty?

4) Using Scripture, describe how God defines true beauty. First Peter 3:3–6 is a great place to start. How is God's definition of beauty different from the way our culture defines beauty?

5) What are some warning signs that you may be too concerned with your outward appearance?

6) Carolyn says, "The way we think about and attend to our personal appearance is really a mirror of our hearts" (p. 38). What did the Heart Check questions on pp. 38–39 show you about your heart?

7) What are some practical ways to fight the tide of culturally-defined beauty and instead seek true beauty in our lives?

8) Carolyn urges us to "acknowledge God's providence and receive with gratefulness the body and appearance he has given to us" (p. 41). In what area(s) have you found that difficult?

9) How should the truths that your body is created by God and a temple of the Holy Spirit affect the way you live?

10) Read 1 Timothy 2:9–10. What heart attitudes are to characterize Christian women? How should those heart attitudes be expressed outwardly? What bearing should this passage have on a woman's dress and physical appearance, as well as her heart motivations?

11) Would you say that you are more intentional about pursuing true beauty or outward beauty? What is one practical way you could cultivate "the imperishable beauty of a gentle and quiet spirit" (1 Pet. 3:4)? Ask God to reveal and set you free from any idolatrous focus on self, so you can experience the freedom of living to glorify God and please Christ.

CHAPTER 3: DADDY'S GIRL

1) What movie or piece of literature embodies what you think of as the ideal father? What traits do you like about the father who is portrayed?

2) What thoughts and feelings does the word *father* bring to mind for you? (They could be positive or negative, based on your experiences.)

3) Read 2 Corinthians 6:16, 18. God calls himself our Father. What does that term imply about God's nature and our relationship with him?

4) Christianity is the only religion in which followers enter into an intimate family relationship with their God. J. I. Packer wrote, "If you want to judge how well a person understands Christianity, find out how much he makes of the thought of being God's child, and having God as his Father." Why is this teaching so central to the gospel?

5) How does Jesus point us to the Father-heart of God?

6) Read Romans 8:15–16. How does our adoption into God's family affect day-to-day living? What is different about your life because you are able to call God "Father"? (Or, if you are not yet a member of God's family, what do you think would change if you were to become a child of God?)

7) How should a deep understanding that God is our Father affect the way we view confession and repentance?

8) How should an understanding that God is our Father affect the way we view suffering and sacrifice?

9) How would you describe your relationship with your heavenly Father? How could you nurture a deeper love relationship with him?

10) Spend some time praying for a deeper understanding of your heavenly Father's love for you. Meditate on 1 John 3:1 and Romans 8:14–17.

CHAPTER 4: PORTRAIT OF A WOMAN USED BY GOD

1) If you were meeting someone for the first time and trying to describe yourself, what are three things you would say to define your identity?

2) Nancy listed eighteen characteristics of Mary of Nazareth (summarized on pp. 77–78). Which of these qualities particularly ministered to you? Why?

3) Read the account of Mary found in Luke 1:26–38 (found on p. 64). Why do you think God chose Mary to be the mother of Jesus?

4) What did Mary suffer as a result of her surrender to God's will?

5) Nancy says that God has chosen all of us (whether or not we are mothers) to bear and nurture spiritual life (see John 15:16). How could a woman without biological children fulfill that calling? How well are you fulfilling this call right now?

6) What prerequisites must be present in order for us to carry out God's purpose for our lives? In other words, what is our part in fulfilling what God has called us to do?

7) What impossible task has God called you to? What promises has he given to help you fulfill that call?

8) Nancy discusses the need to have quiet in our lives in order to hear God's voice. How do you maintain a quiet heart in the busyness of life? Are there new habits you'd like to cultivate in this area?

9) Mary's life was characterized by submission—to God and then to her husband and finally to her Son. Can you think of a time when you submitted

control of something and God worked out the details even better than you could have imagined? Share your experience.

10) How does Mary's life stand in contrast to the world's perspective on womanhood?

11) What steps do you need to take in order to be better prepared to fulfill God's calling and mission for your life? Reread the questions on pp. 77–78 as you meditate on areas in which God wants to mold you so he can use you for his kingdom purposes in this world.

CHAPTER 5: BECOMING A WOMAN OF DISCRETION

1) What are some examples in our culture of the powerful influence of women, for good and for bad?

2) Proverbs 14:1 tells us that the wise woman builds her house but the foolish woman tears down her house with her own hands. What are some ways women "tear down" their house? (Think of a woman's "house" as her immediate sphere of influence.)

3) What are you doing to "build" your house? What are you doing that could be "tearing it down"?

4) What cautions and warnings does Proverbs 7 provide for young men?

5) Describe the difference between a woman who morally is like a "wall" and one who is like a "door" (see p. 81). How does our culture encourage women to be like a "door"? What would motivate a woman to become like a "wall"?

6) Walk through Proverbs 7 and point out the marks of a foolish woman. Look for how she uses her tongue, her attitudes, and her behavior, both in relation to her husband and outside her marriage.

7) Do you see a tendency toward any of these characteristics in your life? Are there any heart attitudes or behaviors for which you need to repent?

8) The foolish woman in Proverbs 7 sacrifices long-term gain to indulge in immediate self-gratification. You may not have seduced a man as she did, but can you think of a time when you have satisfied selfish impulses with no regard for the long-term consequences? Share as you are comfortable, ei-

ther theoretical examples of "what women do" or examples of shortsighted choices you personally have made.

9) If you are married, how can you learn from the foolish women of Proverbs 7 and build your house even if your "needs" aren't being met?

10) If you are single, what cautions and lessons can you learn from the example of the Proverbs 7 woman?

11) God has given women the power to influence men in a unique way. Pray about how you can use that influence wisely, in a way that "builds your house." Are there any specific steps or changes God is calling you to make? The self-assessment questions on pp. 94–95 are helpful to consider as you pray through these issues.

CHAPTER 6: PRUNED TO BLOOM

1) Describe what gardeners do to care for their plants. What does a neglected garden look like?

2) Read John 15:1–8. According to this passage, why does God prune us? What is his goal? What forms might that pruning take?

3) Pruning can be painful. Why is it necessary? Why is it worth submitting to the process? What is our part in the pruning process? Describe what that looks like in real life.

4) Bunny states that we are usually in one of three places: we have just been pruned, we are growing back after a pruning, or we are in full bloom. Where do you find yourself right now? Explain.

5) What circumstance(s) in your life are you tempted to try to control rather than being willing for God to work his will in the situation? Why is it important for you to relinquish control to God—what happens in us when we stop trying to control things?

6) What kind of fruit is evident in the life of a well-pruned woman? Share an example of a woman you know whose life has been made more fruitful through the pruning process.

7) Meditate on your response to God's pruning in your life. Is there a struggle that he is trying to use to bring you into greater fruitfulness? What steps can you take to open yourself to his pruning rather than resisting it?

CHAPTER 7: A WIFE'S RESPONSIBILITY TO HELP HER HUSBAND

1) What are some ingredients or qualities that our culture considers important aspects of a successful marriage?

2) What impressed you about Barbara's account of her parents? How did her mother "adorn" the gospel of Jesus Christ in her calling as a wife? By today's standards, her mother's faithfulness over the long haul would be considered unthinkable, even foolish. What dividends did she reap from the tough choices she made?

3) How should Christian marriages reflect the relationship between Christ and his bride, the church?

4) How might God's order for marriage, with the husband as the head and the wife as a "suitable helper" who is equal but different alleviate many of the marital problems you see in marriages around you or in society at large?

5) Read 1 Peter 2:21–3:1, which offers a beautiful picture of Christ's submission. What phrases in this passage describe submission? How is this definition of submission different from the world's definition?

6) Following Christ's example in the above passage, where can we find the power to submit in a difficult situation?

7) Barbara says, "Submission to our husbands begins and ends with trusting God" (p. 117). Discuss the relationship between submission and trust in God: how does faith enable us to submit to God-ordained authorities? How is submission an expression of faith?

8) First Peter 3:3-6 goes on to further define the particular way women are to submit to their husbands. We are to be characterized by gentleness— "strength under control." Describe what this type of submission might look like in the situation of a wife who disagrees with her husband about, say, a major purchase or a decision in relation to their children.

9) Barbara quotes a sermon that clarifies how Sarah submitted to Abraham: "She lived with a flawed man who asked her to do something unthinkable, yet she didn't hold his horrendous failure over him the rest of his life but restored her respect for him in her heart and lived with him, calling him, 'Master'" (p. 121). If you are married, what is one area where you need to show greater respect for your husband, regardless of whether he "deserves" respect?

10) How can a deeper understanding of submission in marriage help you better submit to God, whether you are married or single?

11) Think and pray about any barriers that are preventing you from the life of submission you've been called to. Are you able to see submission as a gift, or does the term threaten your sense of self-worth?

12) How does Barbara summarize her goal in life as a wife (p. 123)? What is your goal in life as a wife?

CHAPTER 8: LIBERATED THROUGH SUBMISSION

1) Do the words *liberated* and *submitted* seem compatible? Why or why not?

2) Bunny describes what life was like when she "acted" submissive to her husband but wasn't really submitting in her heart—she calls it "dutiful submission." Can you think of a time in your life when you "acted" submissive but it wasn't from your heart? How did that work out? Did anyone notice your insincerity?

3) Women often struggle with the idea of submission. Why does this word get such a bad rap? How are people (wrongly) defining *submission* that makes it so unappealing?

4) Sketch out the biblical "flowchart" of authority. Where do you fit in? Who do you submit to, and who submits to you?

5) How is the principle of submission a blessing and a gift? What are some of the benefits of living by this principle, whether in the home, the church, the workplace, or society?

6) Bunny gives three steps for how to deal with an unreasonable request: stop, speak in truth, and wait on God. Is this a natural reaction for you, or is it a struggle? What reminders could you put in place to help you slow down and respond appropriately instead of getting angry when you are provoked?

7) How can practicing biblical submission result in blessing even when those in authority make mistakes or poor decisions?

8) If you think of submission as "God intervenes," how will your attitude toward submission change? How is this type of submission liberating, as the chapter title suggests?

9) Ideally, when we disagree with our husband, employer, or pastor, we know that "the goal is not to prove who is right and who is wrong, but to discover the will of God on the matter" (p. 132). Think of the last disagreement you had with a human authority. Was your goal to be proved right, or to discover God's will? How did your motivation or goal affect your actions? If you could relive the situation, what would you do differently?

10) Bunny says, "Submission is the pathway He has designed to provide the greatest possible freedom and blessing for every believer" (p. 135). Are you experiencing the freedom and blessing of walking in submission? Confess any area where you have been resisting God-ordained authority. Pray that you will learn to entrust yourself to God and wait for him to intervene.

CHAPTER 9: HOW TO RAISE FEMININE DAUGHTERS

1) If your teenage daughter asked you why women need men and vice versa—how they are different from one another (besides the obvious)—how would you answer her?

2) Feminists argue that equality means sameness and that women must be liberated from slavery to husband and family. How would you respond to this worldview, using God's Word as your reference point?

3) Susan reminds us that our value and identity lie in the fact that we are image bearers of the God of glory. How does this understanding protect us from seeking significance in the wrong place? Think of specific situations in which we or our daughters may be tempted to seek significance in our appearance or our performance.

4) Susan explains that we are products of our theology. Give some examples of how our worldview as women is determined by our belief system.

5) Woman's role as "helper" is elevated by the fact that God and the Holy Spirit are both called Helper. This role for women can take on different meanings for different women and for the same woman in different seasons of her life. But there are some underlying characteristics that cut across all these differences. With that in mind, describe the ways in which our helper design is the same for women across the centuries. What are women uniquely gifted to do, regardless of their vocation or avocation, whether or not they are married, that is different from what men are called to do?

6) Susan writes, "Domesticity means that we prepare safe places where troubled hearts can find rest and comfort, and we involve our daughters in this

ministry in our homes and in our churches" (p. 144). Is this definition of domesticity a new idea for you? Meditate on the feminine virtue of creating a place of rest and comfort for others. What are some practical ways women can express this virtue?

7) How are you accomplishing the virtue of domesticity, and how might God be calling you to do more in this area? You can't create rest for others if you are not peaceful yourself. Pray that God will develop more peace and gentleness in your heart.

8) Why is it crucial that Christian woman pass a legacy of biblical woman-hood on to the women of the next generation? What is at stake? How could you be more intentional about passing on the virtue of true femininity to the next generation, either to your own daughters or to daughters in your church or community?

9) How would you express the essence of a "true woman"?

CHAPTER 10: NURTURING MOTHERS

1) What is one positive childhood memory you have of your mother?

2) Dorothy says that every woman, married or single, has a God-given mater-nal instinct that "is an essential part of his plan for reproducing his heart in the next generation" (p. 151). In what ways does our culture devalue this maternal spirit? Why do you think our world attaches less value to moth-erhood than God does? What role can godly mothers play in God's great redemptive plan?

3) How has God called you to nurture life? If you have children of your own, list additional ways, beyond your own children, that you have been given the opportunity to nurture spiritual life in others.

4) Abortion has become an accepted option in our culture today. What bibli-cal principles affirm the sanctity of human life, beginning in the womb? Use Scripture references if you can. Some women in your group may have experienced the pain of having an abortion, so be sensitive to that possibil-ity as you discuss this topic.

5) What insights from the study of Hannah in this chapter did you find par-ticularly helpful, encouraging, or challenging?

6) Read Hannah's prayer in 1 Samuel 1:10–11. What phrases in her prayer express faith? What is the sequence of her prayer? What heading might you give to each section?

7) Hannah asked for a son so she could give him back to the Lord. If you have children of your own, do you think of your children as your own, or as the Lord's? What specific things might be involved in you giving your child to the Lord? What might keep women from fully consecrating their children to the Lord? How might Hannah's prayer inform your own prayers for your children—either those who call you mother or those you have been called to nurture who are not your own?

8) What aspects of God's character can be best communicated by a nurturing mother? How can you communicate those things to those whom you nurture?

9) Read Hannah's second prayer in 1 Samuel 2:1–10. The seeds of her faith expressed before Samuel's birth have now come to fruition. List all the things she praises God for, and offer up your own prayer of praise for the privilege of nurturing life and giving it back to the Lord.

10) How were Hannah's faith and sacrifice rewarded? What are some of the blessings and rewards of fulfilling "our holy calling to be givers and nurturers of life and [giving] back to his service those whom he has entrusted to our care" (p. 160)?

CHAPTER 11: OLDER WOMEN MENTORING YOUNGER WOMEN

1) Name one or more older women who have influenced your life in a significant way. Describe the nature of your relationship and their influence. What did you learn from them?

2) Read Titus 2:3–5. What is the purpose of the mandate Paul gives Titus in this passage? Why is it so vital for the church to call and equip women for this ministry?

3) Susan says, "Everywhere I go I meet young women who long for spiritual mothers" (p. 162). Why do you think there is not more spiritual mentoring taking place between older and younger women? What are some of the hindrances to this kind of Titus 2 ministry?

4) What is the prerequisite to spiritual mentoring, based on Titus 2:3?

5) What can you gain from a mentoring relationship that you can't get from simply being taught doctrine in a church or classroom setting? What is different about both the method and the outcome?

6) Susan states that every woman is both a younger and an older woman. On a practical level, how might you fit into those two roles?

7) Without engaging in church-bashing, how is your church doing at providing opportunities for mentoring relationships to take place? Is there intentionality in this area? If you don't think your church is strong in this area, how could you improve the situation? (pp. 167–70 offer practical tips for beginning a Titus 2 ministry in your church).

8) How well are you fulfilling the Titus 2 mentoring mandate? Do you need to look for an older woman to mentor you? Where can you start? If you are not currently investing in the life of a younger woman, what can you do to begin such a relationship? If you have been mentored by someone, take a few minutes to write a note thanking her for investing in your life.

NOTES

INTRODUCTION

1. *Time,* "Women: The Road Ahead," Fall 1990.
2. Ibid., 4.
3. Ibid., 76.
4. Ibid., 79.

CHAPTER 1: FEMININITY

1. Version published by Shakespeare.com, copyright © 2000 by Dana Spradley, publisher of Shakespeare.com. Originally derived from the Complete Moby™ Shakespeare, now in the public domain.
2. Author summary of *Femininity* by Susan Brownmiller, as published on Susan-Brownmiller.com, an author-generated web site.
3. Susan Brownmiller, *Femininity* (New York: Fawcett Columbine, 1985).
4. John Piper and Wayne Grudem, eds., *Recovering Biblical Manhood and Womanhood: A Response to Evangelical Feminism* (Wheaton, IL: Crossway Books, 1991), 36.
5. Douglas Wilson, *Reforming Marriage* (Moscow, ID: Canon Press, 1995), 19.
6. Elisabeth Elliot, "Virginity," Elisabeth Elliot Newsletter, March/April 1990 (Ann Arbor, MI: Servant Publications), 1. Requoted by John Piper in the foreword to *Recovering Biblical Manhood and Womanhood,* xxv.
7. Mary Pride, *The Way Home: Beyond Feminism, Back to Reality* (Wheaton, IL: Crossway Books, 1985), 202.

CHAPTER 2: TRUE BEAUTY

1. The American Society of Plastic Surgeons' (ASPS) media summary, issued August 18, 2000 by the ASPS media center.
2. "Reshaping the World" sidebar summary by Mac Margolis, Paige Bierma, Mahion Meyer, Hideko Takayama, and Shehnaz Suterwalia, in *Newsweek International* (Atlantic edition), August 16, 1999, 38.
3. Robin Marantz Henig, "The Price of Perfection," *The Journal of Biblical Counseling,* vol. 15, no. 2, Winter 1997, 34–38. The article originally appeared in the May/June 1996 issue of *Civilization* and was reprinted with permission.
4. Ibid., 35.
5. John Piper, *A Godward Life: Savoring the Supremacy of God in All of Life,* vol. 2 (Sisters, OR: Multnomah, 1999), 64.

CHAPTER 3: DADDY'S GIRL

1. Tamala M. Edwards, "Flying Solo," *Time* (August 28, 2000), 37–43.

2. David Blankenhorn, *Fatherless America: Confronting Our Most Urgent Social Problem* (New York: HarperCollins, 1995), 1.

3. Ibid., 3.

4. J. I. Packer, *Knowing God* (Kent, Great Britain: Hodder and Stoughton, 1975), 224.

5. Bob Carlisle, *Butterfly Kisses: Tender Thoughts Shared Between Fathers and Daughters* (Nashville: Countryman Books, 1997), iv.

6. John MacArthur, *The MacArthur New Testament Commentary: Romans 1–8* (Chicago: Moody, 1991), 436–37.

7. Ibid., 437.

CHAPTER 4: PORTRAIT OF A WOMAN USED BY GOD

1. Kathleen White, *John and Betty Stam* (Minneapolis: Bethany, 1989), 118.

2. From a message called "The Maximum Man" by Adrian Rogers, preached at a Maximum Manhood Conference at Bellevue Baptist Church, Memphis, on October 10, 1985.

3. W. E. Vine, *The Expanded Vine's Expository Dictionary of New Testament Words*, ed. John R. Kohlenberger III with James A. Swanson (Minneapolis: Bethany, 1984), 617.

CHAPTER 5: BECOMING A WOMAN OF DISCRETION

1. *The Words of John Adams, Second President of the United States: With a Life of the Author, Notes and Illustrations, by His Grandson Charles Francis Adams*, vol. 3 (Boston: Charles C. Little and James Brown, 1851), 171.

2. *Strong's Exhaustive Concordance* (Grand Rapids, MI: Baker, 1992).

CHAPTER 7: A WIFE'S RESPONSIBILITY TO HELP HER HUSBAND

1. Philip D. Jensen and Tony Payne, *Beyond Eden* (Sydney, Australia: St. Matthias Press, 1990), 33.

2. Wendy Shalit, *A Return to Modesty* (New York: Simon and Schuster, 1999), 139–40.

3. Kirsten Birkett, "Reopening a Window," *The Briefing*, 159/60, June 20, 1995, 2.

4. Jensen and Payne, *Beyond Eden*, 19.

5. Claire Smith, "Two Commands to Women," *The Briefing*, 159/60, June 20, 1995, 16.

6. Wayne Grudem, *Systematic Theology* (Downers Grove, IL: InterVarsity, 1994), 249–50.

7. Barbara Brotman, "Matter of Roles," (WomanNews), *Chicago Tribune*, October 11, 2000, 2.

8. Colin Brown, *The New International Dictionary of New Testament Theology*, vol. 2 (Grand Rapids, MI: Zondervan, 1979), 256–57.

9. William Barclay, *A New Testament Wordbook* (New York: Harper, n.d.), 103.

10. Ibid., 104.

11. James Johnston, from a sermon delivered at College Church, Wheaton, IL, September 13, 1998.

Notes

CHAPTER 8: LIBERATED THROUGH SUBMISSION

1. Laura Doyle, *The Surrendered Wife* (New York: Fireside; Simon and Schuster, 1999, 2001).

CHAPTER 9: HOW TO RAISE FEMININE DAUGHTERS

1. *The Westminster Confession of Faith, Together with the Larger Catechism and the Shorter Catechism* (Atlanta: Presbyterian Church in America Committee for Christian Education & Publications, 1990).
2. Danielle Crittenden, *What Our Mothers Didn't Tell Us* (New York: Simon and Schuster, 1999), 25.
3. Susan Hunt, *By Design* (Wheaton, IL: Crossway Books, 1994), 101, 108, 171, 173.
4. John Angell James, *Female Piety* (London: Hamilton Adams, 1860; repr., Morgan, PA: Soli Deo Gloria, 1994), 75.
5. Hunt, *By Design*, 118.
6. Louis Berkhof and Cornelius Van Til, *Foundations of Christian Education: Addresses to Christian Teachers*, ed. Dennis E. Johnson (Phillipsburg, NJ: P&R, 1990; orig. Grand Rapids, MI: Eerdmans, 1953), 77.
7. John Angell James, *A Help to Domestic Happiness* (London: Frederick Westley and A. H. Davis, 1833; repr., Morgan, PA: Soli Deo Gloria, 1995), 128–29
8. Susan Hunt, *The True Woman* (Wheaton, IL: Crossway Books, 1997), 22, 34–35.

CHAPTER 11: OLDER WOMEN MENTORING YOUNGER WOMEN

1. Susan Hunt, *Spiritual Mothering: The Titus 2 Model for Women Mentoring Women* (Wheaton, IL: Crossway Books, 1992), 39–40.
2. Ibid., 12.
3. W. E. Vine, *An Expository Dictionary of New Testament Words*, vol. 4 (Old Tappan, NJ: Revell, 1940), 44.
4. For more information call: 1-800-283-1357.

GENERAL INDEX

McCheyne, Robert Murray, 39
Magnificat, Mary's, 70
Male leadership, 26, 27
Marriage, 15, 26, 27, 94, 103, 109,
    112, 113, 116, 130, 155
    companionship in, 27, 28
    leadership in, 26, 115, 116
    marriage vows, 113
    oneness in, 144
    order in, 115, 116, 123
    respect for husband in, 113, 115,
        121, 122, 123, 124
    roles in, 113, 114, 115
    submission in. See *Submission in
        marriage*
    unity in, 114
Mary of Nazareth, mother of Jesus,
    63, 159
Masculine and feminine (male and
    female), distinctions or differ-
    ences between, 25, 80, 113, 114,
    115, 116, 122, 123, 141, 144
Maternal instinct, 151
Maternity. See *Motherhood*
Media, the, 35, 71, 79, 89
Men of Issachar, the, 148
Miller, Charles, 35
Modesty, 41, 43, 44, 80, 86, 95
Moses, 142
Motherhood, 29, 151, 154, 156,
    157, 158, 160
    calling of, 30
    motherhood meltdown, 30
Motives. See *Heart*
Much Ado About Nothing (Shake-
    speare), 23

Older women teaching younger
    women, 31, 81, 161
"One flesh," 114, 155

Packer, J. I., 51
Patience, 133, 134
Paul, the apostle, 113
Peninnah, 154, 155, 156

Piper, John, 25, 41
Pluralism, 161
Postmodern culture, 137, 162
Prayer, 19, 31, 38, 57, 69, 70, 74,
    78, 93, 143, 146, 157, 158, 166,
    167, 169, 170
Proverbs 31 woman, the, 31, 40,
    41, 90
Pruning, spiritual, 100, 101
Purity, 65, 77, 82, 95

Raising feminine daughters, 137
Rebekah, 37
Redemption, God's redemptive pur-
    poses, 39, 40, 63, 65, 67, 70, 76,
    77, 115, 130, 138, 143, 144, 145
Relationships, 15, 25, 26, 50, 90,
    94, 95, 113, 114, 130, 159, 162,
    163, 164, 165, 167, 168, 169
Relativism, 137
Remarriage, 17
Return to Modesty, A (Shalit), 113
Revival, 69
"Rock of Ages" (Toplady), 66
Rogers, Adrian, 69

Samson, 91
Samuel, 159
Sanctification, 140
Sarah, 37, 44, 45, 120, 121, 154
Schaeffer, Edith, 32
Schaeffer, Dr. Francis, 32
Seductresses, adulteresses, tempt-
    resses, 82, 85, 86, 91
Self, 43, 102, 104
Self-gratification, 89
Serial divorce, 17
Servanthood, 30, 68, 94
    servant leadership, 26
Sexual revolution, the, 113
Shakespeare, 23, 24
Shalit, Wendy, 113, 114
Simeon, 75
Sin, 76, 77, 84, 88, 90, 139, 143

SCRIPTURE INDEX